Forth and Clyde Canal

(EXTINGUISHMENT OF RIGHTS OF NAVIGATION) ACT, 1962

The British Transport Commission HEREBY GIVE NOTICE as follows :—

Under Section 1 of the above mentioned Act all Rights of Navigation on the main Forth and Clyde Canal from its Junctions with the Junction Dock and the Carron Dock (including the Timber Basins on each side of Earls Road), all in the Burgh of Grangemouth in the County of Stirling to its termination at the foot of the Locks connecting the Canal with the River Clyde and with Bowling Harbour in the Parish of Old Kilpatrick, in the County of Dunbarton, and on the Glasgow Arm from its commencement by a junction with the main Forth and Clyde Canal south east of Stockingfield Aqueduct to its termination with the Monkland Canal at Castle Street Bridge, all in the City of Glasgow, will be extinguished on the 1st of January 1963.

That on and after the 1st day of January 1963, no vessel will be permitted to navigate or lie in the above mentioned lengths of Canal and that all vessels must be removed therefrom not later than 31st December 1962.

Dated this 24th day of October 1962.

G. B. LAKIN,
Manager,
Forth and Clyde, Monkland
and Union Canals

Old Basin Works,
Applecross Street,
Glasgow, C.4.

A private boating party at Linlithgow.
Judy Gray.

Scotland's
Millennium Canals
The survival and revival of
the Forth & Clyde and Union Canals

Passengers on the pleasure steamer *Fairy Queen* (2).

Guthrie Hutton

Stenlake Publishing 2002

© Guthrie Hutton 2002
First Published in the United Kingdom, 2002 by Stenlake Publishing
Telephone/Fax: 01290 551122

ISBN 1 84033 181 X

The publishers regret that they cannot supply copies of any pictures featured in this book.

To Aunt Eileen
A West End lady who introduced a wild colonial boy to a canal
that became an obsession when 'they' closed it.

The lodge cottage for South Bantaskine House seen through the arch of Bantaskine Bridge on the Union Canal, Falkirk.

Endpapers
The Forbes trustees commissioned Alexander Nasmyth to produce a drawing to show the impact of the nasty, dirty, industrial canal on the genteel amenity of Callendar House. The exaggerated depiction looks faintly ridiculous to modern eyes, but it had the desired effect of persuading Parliament to refuse permission for the canal to be cut through the estate.
Bob McCutcheon.

Contents

Expression of Appreciation

I am indebted to a host of people for their help in compiling this book.

The staffs at libraries and archives across Scotland have helped enormously, sometimes without knowing it, and I am very grateful to all those at William Patrick Library, Kirkintilloch; the West Lothian Library Headquarters, Blackburn; Clydebank Library; the Mitchell Library and Glasgow City Archives; Falkirk Library; Falkirk Museums, Callendar House; Edinburgh City Library; the Royal Commission on the Ancient and Historical Monuments of Scotland; the National Archives of Scotland, West Register House.

A number of individuals have also helped with advice and illustrations, and I am most grateful to them. Brian Skillen made his carefully compiled research available to me—it was worth its weight in gold. William B. Black's excellent research into shipbuilding was also of great value. Bob McCutcheon provided his usual enthusiasm and splendid material, and David Smith's information on curling added an interesting aspect to the story. James Dunn's local mining knowledge was also helpful. I have to thank *The Link* newsletter for putting me in touch with George Bergius who was very helpful with information and pictures from the family firm. The *Falkirk Herald* also helped to put me in touch with Effie Mallice, Malcolm Allan and Ronald MacIntyre. Hugh McGinley helped with advice on canoeing, and Margaret Heriot and Elizabeth Thomson supplied some excellent photographs.

Much of the story from the later periods came from my often flawed personal memories of a remarkable thirty-plus years of campaigning and I have to thank many colleagues from that time for their help in keeping me right, in particular: Judy Gray, who also produced a wonderful photograph, as did George MacAngus and David Holgate who provided a few, Sandra Purvis, Ronnie Rusack, Tommy and Nancy Lawton, Richard Davies, Helen Rowbotham of British Waterways and my old drouthy cronie Donald Mackinnon who also came up trumps with some pictures.

I should also pay tribute to all those campaigners who, over the years, worked, kicked, scratched, fought and argued their case until the canals were brought back to life. It is their effort, and the work of those in council offices and British Waterways who took up the fight through the 1980s and 90s, that provided the story.

Pleasure steamer *May Queen* at Cadder.

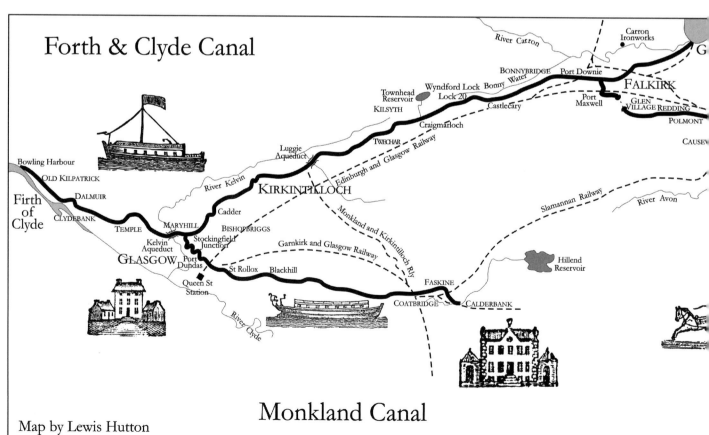

Forth & Clyde Canal

Carron Ironworks

River Carron

BONNYBRIDGE   Port Downie

FALKIRK

Townhead Reservoir   Wyndford Lock   Bonny Water
KILSYTH   Lock 20   Port
                                    Castlecary   Maxwell   GLEN
                                                                VILLAGE REDDING
                            Craigmarloch   POLMONT

Luggie   TWECHAR   CAUSEW
Aqueduct   Edinburgh and Glasgow Railway

Bowling Harbour

OLD KILPATRICK

DALMUIR   River Kelvin   KIRKINTILLOCH   Slamannan Railway   River Avon

Firth
of
Clyde   CLYDEBANK   Cadder
                                            Monkland and Kirkintilloch Rly
         TEMPLE   MARYHILL   BISHOPBRIGGS
              Kelvin   Stockingfield
              Aqueduct   Junction   Garnkirk and Glasgow Railway   Hillend
GLASGOW   Port   Reservoir
              Dundas   St Rollox   Blackhill
         Queen St   FASKINE
         Station   COATBRIDGE   CALDERBANK

River Clyde

Monkland Canal

Map by Lewis Hutton

Coal scow at Ratho gasworks.

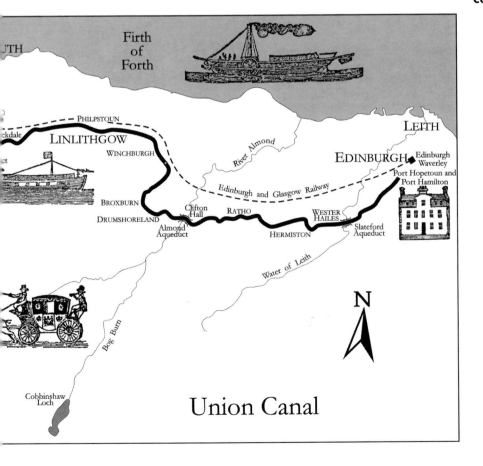

Union Canal

Bascule bridge mechanism

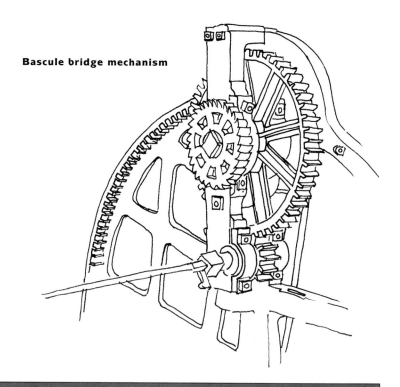

Dalmuir Bridge

blether at the bridge

The canal bridge, like the street corner, was a place where men gathered to settle world affairs, or just have a blether, as here at Dalmuir where the first 'traditional' bascule bridge may have been installed. The original 'drawbridges' had decks lifted by chains attached to overhead ballast beams—like those over medieval castle moats or Dutch canals. Cattle often refused to cross them, so Highland drovers disliked them. It was important to solve the problem for Dalmuir Bridge because it carried the main road west of Glasgow.

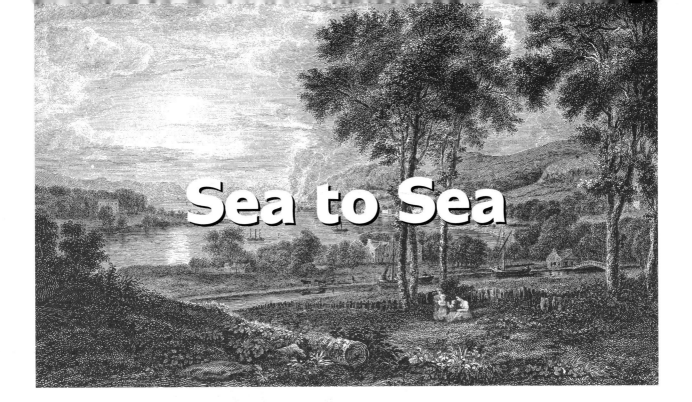

Sea to Sea

The Clyde from Dalnottar Hill with the canal in the foreground.

Scotland started the eighteenth century as a poor country, and it stayed poor thanks to the turmoil surrounding the Act of Union and the disruption of two Jacobite rebellions. Then, in the second half of the century, the nation shook off its demons and entered an extraordinary age of creativity and innovation known as 'the Enlightenment'. This is usually typified by the work of great thinkers, artists and architects, but the period's achievements also include two massive industrial enterprises: the Carron Ironworks and the Forth & Clyde Canal. Remarkably, both were based on the twisting, turning, tidal River Carron.

Carron Ironworks was set up by the Carron Company in 1760 about four miles from the river's confluence with the Forth estuary. Water from the river was diverted into the works to provide power, and the river itself gave access to the sea for shipping finished products out and raw materials in. Coal and ironstone were abundant at Bo'ness and, if an alternative fuel was needed, there were extensive birch woods nearby for making charcoal. Three miles downstream, at the point where the Grange Burn joined the narrow, muddy river, was where the canal's sea lock was built.

Schemes and Scheming

Proposals to cut a canal across the narrow neck of central Scotland were not new. King Charles II thought it would give his navy a strategic advantage and although the route was surveyed, nothing further was done. The same fate was shared by other surveys in the first half of the eighteenth century, but this idea's time had come when John Smeaton was asked to prepare a survey for a ship canal in 1763. He looked at two routes, one between Stirling and Loch Lomond and a cheaper, more direct line through the Carron and Kelvin Valleys. This direct route also ran well to the west of Glasgow, which annoyed the city's merchants. They wanted a canal from the city to the east coast so that they could take in goods from America and Europe and re-export them and, while others talked, they acted. In 1766 they commissioned a survey from Scottish

Weir and take-off point for the feeder from the
Bothlin Burn at Craigenbay, Lenzie.

The Luggie Aqueduct at Kirkintilloch with the
later Campsie Branch Railway.

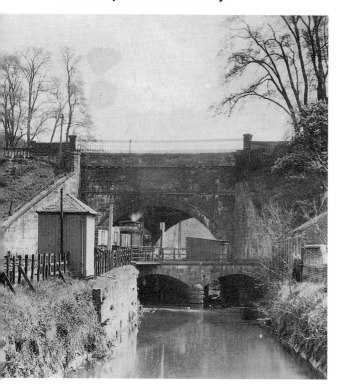

engineer Robert Mackell, but his first scheme was too expensive and so, in collaboration with James Watt (of steam engine fame), he surveyed another route based on Smeaton's plan. It was not suitable for seagoing ships, only barges, but it was what the merchants wanted and they presented a bill to Parliament seeking the authority to go ahead. The plan was supported by the Carron Company and, when a branch canal from Carronshore to Bo'ness was incorporated, it looked to be heading for success.

Supporters of Smeaton's grand design were alarmed at the prospect of the small 'barge canal' being approved, because, if it went ahead, it would gain access to the usable water sources, occupy the best ground, and thus scupper plans for the larger canal. Opposition grew. A struggle developed between east and west, between high ideals and commerce. The small canal's opponents managed to delay its progress through Parliament and commissioned John Smeaton to prepare new plans for a canal, with branches to Glasgow and Bo'ness, capable of taking seagoing vessels. It was the classic compromise and it won the day. The bill for the small canal was withdrawn, and the Act of Parliament authorising the canal that came to be known as the Forth & Clyde was passed on 8 March 1768. Construction began on 10 June when Sir Lawrence Dundas of Kerse, the governor of the Canal Company, dug the first spadeful of earth on the site of the sea lock.

Most of Scotland cheered, but Bo'ness was worried and with good reason. The branch canal the town had fought for was started, but never completed. Meanwhile a village grew up beside the Forth & Clyde's sea lock and, as the years passed, this developed into Grangemouth which rivalled and ultimately overtook Bo'ness as the principal port on the upper Forth.

Townhead Reservoir.

Construction

The canal was a heroic undertaking and it took big men with big ideas to build it. John Smeaton was the engineer; his assistant was one of his earlier rivals, Robert Mackell. Smeaton was based in Yorkshire and sent drawings north to Mackell who had to engage contractors and supervise the work. He was a tough character, not averse to amending Smeaton's plans, and much of the canal as built can be credited to him.[1]

Digging the channel and constructing the bridges, culverts and twenty locks up to the summit level progressed steadily, but when the engineers and navvies pushed west from Lock 20 onto Dullatur Bog they hit a problem. They made repeated attempts to excavate the channel across the unstable ground, but these failed and instead they had to build up artificial embankments and create the channel between them. Earth and stones, piled on beds of willow fascines, sank over 50 feet into the bog before the embankments stabilised, and they continued to settle after that and had to be topped up from time to time.

While work was progressing on the canal itself, men were building a large earth dam to create Townhead Reservoir from where the canal would draw most of its water. It was filled by natural watercourses diverted into it from the Kilsyth Hills. By 1773 the canal was completed to Kirkintilloch and water was let in to allow trade between the east coast and a basin known variously as Kirkintilloch Harbour, Port Hillhead or Hillhead Basin. It was, in effect, Scotland's first man-made inland port where goods bound to and from the sea lock and Glasgow were transshipped between boats and carts.

To the west of Hillhead was the crowning glory so far, the Luggie Aqueduct, a magnificent 50-foot span single arch, 90 feet deep. Nothing like it

Ferrydyke Bridge

blether at the bridge

The Antonine Wall, the Roman Empire's most northerly frontier, crosses the country on a similar line to the one taken by the canal. The two diverge at Cadder and come together again at Old Kilpatrick where Ferrydyke Bridge appears to perpetuate the line of the military way that ran behind the wall. The 'dyke' in the name is thought to be a reference to the Roman wall and 'ferry' to the adjacent crossing of the Clyde.

Kelvin Aqueduct.

had been built in Scotland before and, as if to add to its uniqueness, the contractors, Gibb & Moir from Falkirk, made the arch in three sections. To do it they had to move the wooden centring, on which the stonework was assembled, after each third was completed, but this was done with such skill that the joints where the sections marry are very hard to detect.[2]

Smeaton resigned as engineer in 1773, but not before Mackell had persuaded him to alter the canal's line to bring the summit reach closer to Glasgow, thereby extending its length before any locks would be needed. This saved time and money, although not enough of the latter because the company's funds were running out and in 1775 work stopped at Stockingfield, about three miles from Glasgow. A new basin and warehouses were created, but the city merchants were not satisfied with this and set about raising the capital to make the branch to Hamilton Hill. It was completed in 1777.

Glasgow now had a canal to the east coast augmenting its flourishing Atlantic trade and, with the little upstart city prospering, east coast towns and cities became increasingly agitated as the unfinished canal thwarted their ambitions of reaching the Clyde. They lobbied Parliament which was initially reluctant to bale out a private company, but eventually loaned money from the fund accrued from the resale of forfeited Jacobite estates. Work restarted in 1785 with a new engineer, Robert Whitworth, in charge.

The new man was needed because Smeaton, old and in poor health, had declined the invitation to complete the work and Mackell was dead. Whitworth's greatest achievement was the aqueduct over the River Kelvin at Maryhill; a 400 foot long structure, with four 50-foot arches between massive masonry piers. The foundation stone was laid on 15 June 1787. Gibb & Moir were again the contractors and they used stone from Possil Quarry, near Lambhill Bridge, and lime from Netherwood, to the west of Wyndford Lock (Lock No. 20).

The new section of canal was made deeper than the old and so, to achieve a consistent depth, Whitworth raised the original banks and lowered the lock cills. He also built up the banks through Dullatur Bog and had several reaches run off so that high points could be dredged.

As construction neared completion, anticipation of the grand opening grew. Posters appeared in Glasgow advertising that on 1 April 1790 water would be let into the locks and across the Kelvin Aqueduct, and that a viewing platform would be set up. About 1,000 people turned up to witness the historic occasion, but as the *Caledonian Mercury* reported a week later, they were the victims of an elaborate April Fool![3]

FORTH and CLYDE NAVIGATION

Open from Sea to Sea

NOTICE IS HEREBY GIVEN,

THAT the communication between the Eastern and Western Seas, by means of the Great Canal from the river Forth to the Clyde, is now *completely open* for the navigation of vessels of the draught of 8 feet water or under, and constructed to pass locks 20 feet wide, and about 68 feet long. There being abundance of water for all the purposes of the navigation, there is now no risque of disappointment, delay, or detention, on that account.—The extreme length of the navigation is 35 miles; the lock dues amount to 5 s. 10 d. per ton in all; and the time required to pass from sea to sea, through 39 locks, will be about 16 hours.

Office of Forth and Clyde Navigation,
Glasgow, 6th August, 1790.

Opening

The real opening took place on 28 July 1790 when the Magistrates of Glasgow joined the Canal Company's committee of management on their boat. It took four hours to travel from Glasgow to Bowling, where the vessel was lowered through the sea lock to the Clyde. The chairman, Archibald Spiers of Elderslie, and engineer, Robert Whitworth, poured a hogshead of water from the Forth into the Clyde to symbolise the union of the eastern and western seas. The crowds cheered; the canal was open.[4] A few days later a sloop called *Agnes* made

Ships using the canal in 1801 included:

Felicity, captain Parklington, from Boston (Lincs) to Liverpool with grain.
Mary, captain McLaren, from Limekilns to Limerick with herrings.
Jean, captain Beattie, from Burntisland to Liverpool with grain.
Nelly Packet, captain Kirkland, from Ayr to Queensferry with turpentine.
Joseph and Son, captain Wood, from Leith to Newry with flaxseed and herrings.
Agenoria, captain Windlay, from Bangor to Berwick with slates.
Aberdeen Packet, captain Ritchie, from Montrose to Greenock with goods.
Bruce and Ann, captain Balmain, from Prestonpans to Ireland with vitriol.
Glasgow Packet, captain Robertson, from Port Glasgow to Newcastle with sugars.
Two Brothers, captain Craig, from Liverpool to Anstruther with salt.
James, captain McKie, from Rothesay to Leith with slates.
Friendship, captain McKellar, from Greenock to Leith with kelp.
Perseverance, captain Clay, from Greenock to Hamburg with goods.
Mary, captain Baird, from Stirling to Dumbarton with oak timber.
Peggie, captain Davie, from Limekilns to Greenock with smithy coal.
Potter, captain Barton, from Newcastle to Liverpool with goods.
Isabella, captain Hutton, from Dundee to Liverpool with goods.
Jean, captain Blair, from Dumbarton to London with bottles.
Admiral Duncan, captain Buchanan, from King's Lynn to Dumbarton with sand.
Jean, captain Bain, from Peterborough to Greenock with hemp and iron.
Nancy, captain Kidd, from Liverpool to Dundee with salt.
Countess of Stair, captain Baird, from Greenock to Kincardine with hardware and a return cargo from Kennetpans to Dublin.[5]

Port Dundas: an engraving by Joseph Swan.

City of Glasgow Libraries and Archives;
The Mitchell Library.

City of Glasgow Libraries and Archives; The Mitchell Library.

the first sea-to-sea crossing when she sailed from Leith to Greenock, and in early September the *Mary* sailed in the other direction from Greenock to Grangemouth.[6]

In a favourable wind, seagoing ships could pass along the canal under sail, but usually they required assistance from a tracker. Trackers were people who provided and worked the towing—or tracking—horses, but to begin with there were too few of them with good horses and they exploited their advantage by charging high prices. It was a serious situation which threatened to retard sea-to-sea trade, and so the company came to a financial arrangement with 'approved' trackers who agreed to always have horses available when ships wanted them. Depending on the weather it took anything from two to five horses to haul the heavier sloops and brigs at only two miles an hour, but the speed did not deter the many traders who wanted to use the canal. Roads throughout Scotland were poor, and with almost every sizeable community in the country located on the coast, or by an estuary or navigable river, the canal opened up coastal shipping routes. And it wasn't just Scotland that benefited. East and west coast English ports traded with each other through the canal and trade with Ireland developed.

Port Dundas

The Canal Company expected the completed sea-to-sea link to boost trade, so in 1790 they extended the Glasgow Branch from Hamilton Hill to Hundred Acre Hill, where they created a new terminal basin, Port Dundas. Warehouses were built and a new village was developed alongside. Industry and commerce, attracted by the port's proximity to the city centre, moved in. Trade was also attracted away from the Clyde because boats could be stranded at the Broomielaw at low tide and boat owners sometimes preferred to bring their vessels up to the city by canal.

Glasgow's newspapers reported excitedly on the advantages the canal and its port were bringing to the city. Wheat, barley, sugar, salt, coffee, whale oil, coal, ironstone, iron products, wood from the Baltic and America, tar and ashes from Archangel, and a variety of other goods were all pouring in. Apples from Holland—fresh fruit for the city's growing population—rated a special mention. People who had accepted shortages and high prices as normal saw east coast fishing boats—some from as far north as Banff—bring in seafood in excellent condition and at almost half the normal price.[7]

Regular shipping services were established to destinations such as Dundee, Aberdeen, Newcastle and London, while through services from Greenock called at Port Dundas on their way south to the Thames.[8] Others ventured further, sailing regularly to ports including Hamburg, St Petersburg or Amsterdam and occasionally to destinations such as Lisbon and Trieste. Port Dundas was doing so much trade with the east coast and Europe that it was effectively an east coast port. Wharf names like Rotterdam, Hamburgh, London, Leith and Kirkcaldy

City of Glasgow Libraries and Archives; The Mitchell Library.

Ships under sail passing Bonnybridge.

reflected the port's connections. These east coast links also gave rise to the curious phenomenon of canal-based vessels being dismasted, stranded, wrecked or forced by gales to take refuge in coastal harbours. Some were blown north to Orkney before they could head south.[9] Ships, which were too large for the canal, came into Grangemouth and unloaded their cargoes into lighters—up to four or five were needed for the biggest vessels—and with each being towed by two horses, the goods were in Port Dundas sixteen to eighteen hours later. The trade was impressive and, although overshadowed by the city's transatlantic links, must have had a huge impact on Glasgow's economic growth. With trade going both east and west, Glasgow had effectively become a hub port before the concept was invented.

Visits from royalty added to the European connection: in 1816 His Imperial Highness the Grand Duke Nicholas, brother of the Emperor of Russia, came to see Port Dundas during a tour of Glasgow. Two years later Archduke Maximillian of Austria was a guest at Tennent's chemical works and saw the canal at St Rollox.[10]

But if Port Dundas was significant to Glasgow's progress, it was vital to the canal, accounting for over half of all trade in the early years. Of that, the trade coming into Port Dundas from the east was more than double the combined total of trade with the Clyde and that going to the Forth, and the proportion continued to rise as ships became larger and coast to coast traffic dwindled through the first half of the nineteenth century. New basins were added early in the century and again in the 1840s.[11]

The Monkland Canal

Inland trade developed through Port Dundas along the Monkland Canal as well. This canal had been started in 1770 as a means of bringing coal into Glasgow from the rich coalfields around Coatbridge. It was planned as an isolated inland waterway and completed to a terminal at Germiston, to the east of Glasgow, in 1773. Success eluded it and in an effort to improve its fortunes it was extended, between 1780 and 1783, to the top of Blackhill and from the base of the hill to a point about a mile from Port Dundas. A gravity railway connected the two sections of canal, with coal being unloaded into wagons at the top of the hill and loaded back into barges at the foot. But even these measures did not solve the canal's financial difficulties and on top of that there were serious water supply problems.

The Forth & Clyde was also struggling to cope with the demand for water, despite having developed other sources to supplement its supplies from Townhead Reservoir. The Acts of Parliament for each canal had granted them rights to draw water from designated catchment areas, but the two overlapped. It was a situation that could have got nasty, but instead of engaging in a ruinous competition for the water, the two companies got together and developed a mutually beneficial system.

The Monkland was extended west along what was known as the 'Cut of Junction' from Castle Street to Port Dundas, and east from Coatdyke through two new locks at Sheepford. This eastern cut terminated at Woodhall, Calderbank where the North Calder Water was tapped to fill the new channel. To ensure that this did not deplete the river's flow for other water users, the huge Hillend Reservoir was created at Caldercruix to top it up when required.

Navigation from the coalfields into Glasgow was completed by the construction of a flight of locks at Blackhill, and in August 1793 the first barge

Sheepford Locks, Coatdyke, part of the extension to the Monkland Canal made to bring water into the Forth & Clyde.

Honble Captain Fleming
Cumbernauld

Dr.

To COLIN MACNAB, & Co.

To Freight of *Thirty Packages 2 Junis Wood 70½* £ 10 . 11 . 6
one Cask anns 11 @ ——— 4/- £ — . 4 .

To Charges, *paid at London & account* — — £ 2 . 8 . 10
£ 13 . 4 . 4

 # Hope Keith from London

GRANGEMOUTH,
8 Jany } 1813

Received payment,

 # Colin Macnab & Co

James Adams

**Bill for goods carried between
London and Cumbernauld through
Grangemouth.**

**Regimental colours of the 8th (Canal Corps)
Glasgow Volunteers.**
Royal Highland Fusiliers Regimental Headquarters and Museum.

worked its way down to Glasgow. There was nothing now to stop the abundant supplies of Monkland coal, promised by the canal's first promoters, from reaching the city. Boom times were just around the corner.

The Napoleonic Wars

During the Forth & Clyde Canal's early years the country was at war with Napoleon, and many ships left Port Dundas fully armed to defend themselves. For a day or so they shared the canal with 150 French prisoners of war who were taken by boat to Edinburgh in October 1798 (the officers went by road). They came from the captured squadron that tried to land troops in Ireland with Wolf Tone.[12]

War flared up again in 1803 and this time invasion seemed likely. If it came the French army would have to be repelled by the militia, a force of doubtful ability which recruited by ballot. Men could normally buy themselves out, but when recruiting was increased to meet the threat the only way of avoiding the call-up was to form or join a volunteer regiment. Glasgow raised a troop of light horse and eight foot regiments; one was the 8th (Canal Corps) Glasgow Volunteers.

The corps was formed by the brothers Hugh and Robert Baird who owned the Canal Basin Foundry at Hamilton Hill. Two companies of 60 men mustered in scarlet tunics and blue breeches for their first inspection at the Old Basin in November 1803. Thirty of them had muskets, the rest had pikes and there were also two artillery pieces manned by gunners in blue tunics and white breeches. The corps was presented with full military colours in 1805 and its numbers increased to 240 men, but in that same year Nelson won his famous victory at Trafalgar, the threat of invasion receded and the brave volunteers became irrelevant. Glasgow's units were absorbed into a new Lanarkshire Local Militia in 1809, although the Canal Corps, like all good soldiers, seems just to have faded away.[13]

It is a matter of curiosity that the corps was the only volunteer unit drawn from a single industry, and the Bairds' reasons for setting it up can only be guessed at. They probably wanted to avoid the recruitment ballot themselves, but they also kept many men out of the militia and thereby saved the canal and its related businesses from the serious disruption that would have been caused if a lot of them had been called up. The corps could therefore have been an early attempt to protect a vital industry in time of war. It could also have had a boat named after it; in March 1809 the *Canal Volunteer* passed through Grangemouth on her way from Banton to Leith with a load of coal. She may have belonged to the Baird family whose home was at Kelvinhead, near Banton.

During the real war, the Canal Company exempted Government traffic from paying dues and canal boats were used to move troops between the west and east coasts, while military equipment was brought to Port Dundas to be stored in warehouses. The port's links to the sea were not lost on the Royal Navy whose press-gangs found rich pickings there when they conducted what contemporary papers called a 'hot press'.[14]

For LONDON, direct,
The armed Brig
GLASGOW,
William Nuccle, Master,
One of the Canal London Traders, is now at the Canal Bafon, taking on board goods for London, and will fail the 9th of September.
Any perfon having goods to forward will pleafe fend them to John Gibfon, at his Cellars, Turner's Clofs, Argyll-ftreet. Glafgow, or to the Mafter on board, where receipts will be granted for them. And,
At LONDON,
The CLYDE, William Cochran, Mafter, Taking on board goods at Dice and Smart's Key, for Glafgow, Paifley, Greenock, and all places adjacent.
Canal Bafon, 30th Aug. 1794.

City of Glasgow Libraries and Archives; The Mitchell Library.

Charlotte Dundas

Steam had been used for a variety of purposes for most of the eighteenth century, but it had never driven a boat. That began to change when William Symington, an engineer from Leadhills, was commissioned by Patrick Miller of Dalswinton, Dumfriesshire, to conduct some experiments. The first took place in 1788 on the small loch on Miller's estate. Its modest success persuaded Miller, a shareholder in the Carron Company, to arrange for Symington to be given facilities at the works to develop a new boat. This was tried out on the canal above Lock 16 at Falkirk in December 1789. Another trial was held about two weeks later, but despite being more successful Miller was unimpressed and withdrew his backing.

The Canal Company took up the challenge in 1800 and asked Symington to build a steam tug or 'tracking boat'. Two years, two boats and numerous modifications to the engine later and Symington was ready. The boat, *Charlotte Dundas*, was taken to Glasgow and on 4 January 1803 sailed from Hamilton Hill to Stockingfield where she took the 100-ton *Active* in tow. Watched by a large crowd of people she hauled her back to Port Dundas at three miles an hour.

Another trial was held on 28 March 1803 when *Charlotte Dundas* took the *Active* and *Euphemia* in tow at Lock 20. A strong wind was blowing and no other boats were moving westward, but she defied the elements, towing the combined weight of 130 tons the eighteen and a half miles to Port Dundas in nine hours, fifteen minutes. Symington had built the world's first practical steamboat and could reasonably expect some praise. He did not get it!

A few days later a Canal Company proprietor wrote to the *Glasgow Herald and Advertiser*. He was miffed that he and his fellow proprietors had not received due credit for funding the experiments and poured scorn on what the 'ingenious mechanic' had achieved. More seriously he feared the wash from the paddle wheel would erode the canal banks and clay puddle.

He was not alone. The committee of management withdrew support, *Charlotte Dundas* was never used again and Symington struggled to gain recognition. Insult was added to injury in 1807 when American inventor, Robert Fulton, who had seen Symington's vessel in action, tried out his *Clermont* on the Hudson River. Scotland's failure to recognise its own pioneer allowed him falsely to claim it as the world's first steamboat![17]

PLEASANT, CHEAP, CONVENIENT,
AND
EASY TRAVELLING.

THE GREAT CANAL PASSAGE BOATS will begin to run on MONDAY the 2d of March, and will continue every lawful day, until notice may be given; one of the Boats will leave Port-Dundas precisely at Ten o'clock, and will arrive at Lock No. 15, near Falkirk, at Four o'clock afternoon, the distance being Twenty-five Miles. A BOAT will also depart from Lock No. 16, near Falkirk, at Eleven o'clock forenoon, and will arrive at Port-Dundas at Five o'clock afternoon. The Fare, for the whole passage of Twenty-five Miles, will be FOUR SHILLINGS in the best Cabin, and TWO SHILLINGS in the second Cabin; the intermediate distances agreeably to the Rates in the printed Way Bills; CHILDREN, under a year old, *not to pay any thing*, and from one to seven years of age, to pay only HALF FARE. Each passenger will be allowed 56lbs. weight of Luggage, *free of any charge.*

THE MARKET PASSAGE BOAT

Will start on the same day, viz. MONDAY the 2d of March, at Seven o'Clock in the Morning, from Castle-carry, where the road from Stirling to Glasgow, by Cumbernauld, crosses the Canal; will arrive at Port-Dundas about Eleven o'Clock; will leave Port Dundas on the same day, at Three o'Clock afternoon, and will reach Castlecarry about Seven o'Clock. The Fare, for the whole passage, in the best Cabin, will be THREE SHILLINGS, and ONE SHILLING and SIXPENCE in the second Cabin; the intermediate distances as stated in the Way Bill.

From the great encouragement these Boats met with last Season, every pains has been taken, and no expense spared, to fit them up in an elegant, convenient and comfortable manner.

Canal Office, Glasgow, }
26th Feb. 1812.   }

City of Glasgow Libraries and Archives; The Mitchell Library.

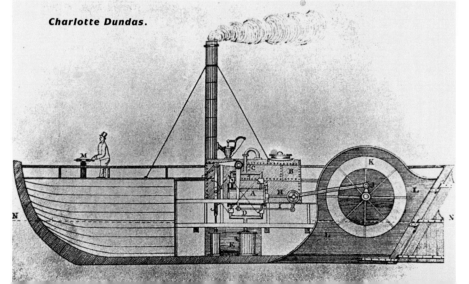

Charlotte Dundas.

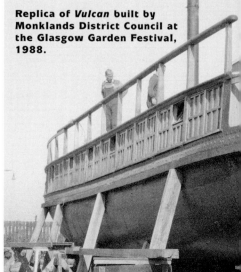

Replica of *Vulcan* built by Monklands District Council at the Glasgow Garden Festival, 1988.

Traffic Management

DEPARTURES AND ARRIVALS
OF THE GREAT CANAL COMPANY'S
Track Boats,
FOR THE CONVEYANCE OF GOODS
Between Grangemouth and Port-Dundas,
AND ALL
INTERMEDIATE PLACES ON THE CANAL.

A BOAT departs from Grangemouth every Monday and Thursday afternoon; goes to Bainsford, or Lock No. 16, that night; leaves No. 16 every Tuesday and Friday morning, at ten o'clock; arrives at Port-Dundas the same evening

Another Boat departs from Port-Dundas every Tuesday and Friday morning, at eight o'clock; goes to Lock No. 16, or Bainsford, that night; arrives at Grangemouth every Wednesday and Saturday morning, at ten o'clock.

There are commodious Wharfs and Warehouses at the different Stages on the Canal. And application may be made to

Robert Virtue & Co. agents, 115, Trongate, Glasgow.
Or at the Track-Boat Office, ...Port-Dundas.
John Barr, Bridge Keeper, ...Hungryside.
John Gray, do. ....Kirkintulloch.
John Shaw, do. ....Auchinstarry.
John Horn, Lock Keeper (Lock No. 20) or Wyndford
Archibald Buchanan, Bridge Keeper, ...Castlecarry.
John Kyle, Lock Keeper, ...Underwood.
Thomas Stark, do. ....Lock No. 16.
William Steven, ...Tophill.
William Bulloch, Bridge Keeper, ...Bainsford.
And any other Lock or Bridge Keeper on the Canal.
William Connochie, Shoremaster, ...Grangemouth.
Thomas Grosart, Track Boat Master, ...Falkirk.
N. B. Regular Trading Lighters leave Port-Dundas, Greenock, and Port-Glasgow, weekly.
Robert Virtue & Co. Agents, ...Glasgow.
Nahan M'Lachlan, Agent, ...Greenock.
Glasgow, 18th May, 1816.

Passenger Boats

It was often far from plain sailing in the early years. A culvert at Whitecrook, Clydebank, collapsed on 11 December 1790 and the canal there was closed until the repair was completed in early January. A few months later, in July 1791, the *Glasgow Advertiser* reported the collapse—and repair in eleven days—of an aqueduct 'about a mile eastward of Old Kilpatrick'.[15] The distance fits with the aqueduct at Duntocher Burn, but according to company records water forcing itself under the puddle had burst open the middle part of Boquhanran Aqueduct before July. Whether one or both gave way is therefore unclear. Not all collapsing tunnels were in the west; a timber tunnel (culvert) at Carmuirs had to repaired three times and another one gave way at Cadder Mill in 1807.

Sections of the canal were closed every summer to carry out repair and maintenance work. It may seem perverse to have shut the canal in high season, but in the days when artificial light was a flickering flame, the extended daylight meant that men could work for as long as they could see. Closures were also kept to a minimum by preparing materials beforehand, and repair locations must have resembled building sites, with stone being delivered, measured, cut, dressed and laid out ready for the appointed day.[16] Inscriptions on some locks testify to the work done during these closures: Lock 18 was 'Rebuilt by AlexR. [Alexander] Easton 1817; Stones from Skipperton Glen' while J. Wyse repaired Lock 5 in 1816 and Lock 14 the following year. Some of the work done was quite extensive, as in the years between 1815 and 1820 when a number of sub-standard locks on the western flight were rebuilt, with whole locksides being taken down and built back up again.

Lock or bridge keepers in those early days had to look after a group of installations, be available 24 hours a day, sweep and clean wharves and attend to loading and unloading. They were permitted to graze animals on the verges, but had to tether them away from the canal's edge after it was found that they could cause damage if they got too close.

The Canal Company started operating track-boats in April 1786. They were slow and cumbersome, and carried all sorts of goods along with luggage and passengers, but it was a new service and people made great efforts to use it. A pregnant woman walked from Linlithgow to Falkirk in May 1790 to catch the Glasgow-bound boat, but the effort proved too much and she died on board.[18] The crews kept up a regular service in all weathers, as in January 1791 when a gale blew the helmsman off the *Lady Catherine*. The master, Michael Johnston, jumped overboard to save the man from drowning and was awarded five guineas by the Canal Company for his heroism. Sadly no one was able to save him when he fell into a lock in 1809 and drowned.[19]

Passage, or passenger, boats started to take over from the all-purpose track-boats in 1809. They operated between Port Dundas and Lock 16 at Camelon and had fires to warm the cabins and a supply of newspapers, books and amusements. Other services developed around them. A market boat left Castlecary Bridge early in the morning for Glasgow, and returned at night. Caravan carts took passengers into Falkirk and Glasgow, and coach services were developed to connect Edinburgh and towns such as Stirling with the boats. The boats operated a reduced service through the winter when the canal was free of ice.

In November 1810 many people drowned when a passage boat capsized on the Glasgow, Paisley & Ardrossan Canal, and the Forth & Clyde Canal

Bonnybridge Aqueduct or Pend

blether at the bridge

The Scottish Radical Reform Movement of 1820 had been infiltrated by Government spies who knew of its plans to form an independent revolutionary government. They also knew of a group of 'radicals' from Glasgow who had set out to meet others from the Falkirk area with the intention of going on to seize cannon from Carron Ironworks. The radicals crossed the canal at Castlecary and some went east along the towpath while the others used the road. They joined up again at Bonnybridge, where they also met a spy who persuaded them to wait for their friends on the Bonnymuir. Instead, about 30 men of the 10th Hussars and Stirlingshire Yeomanry came clattering through Bonnybridge Aqueduct to meet them. The radicals put up a fight, but were easily beaten. Some were taken prisoner, including their leaders John Baird and Andrew Hardie who were later hanged; the others were transported. In April 1981 Winnie Ewing MEP unveiled a plaque at the pend to commemorate the 'battle'.[1]

Bainsford Bridge

blether at the bridge

A van carrying an elephant and rhinoceros from a 'wild beast show' was travelling between Stirling and Falkirk in November 1819. It had to cross the canal at Bainsford because the aqueduct at Camelon was too small. A representative from the show had given the bridge keeper advance warning, and a few hours before the van was due he came to check on arrangements. Nothing had been done, but by chance the Canal Company's carpenter was at the bridge and he scoffed at the idea that it would not take the weight. His confidence no doubt evaporated as the bridge collapsed, but by good fortune the van was longer than the opening and it sat down on the stone abutments. The elephant and rhino were led to safety, but both canal and road had to be closed for repairs. The Canal Company recovered some of the loss by docking the carpenter's wages. They thought it would do him some good if it curtailed his excessive fondness for strong drink! Barges were later put under bridges to support them when heavy loads were going over.[2]

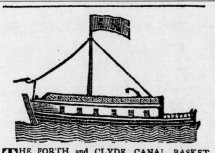

Company was quick to place advertisements in the papers to reassure people that their boats were safe. Passengers may have thought otherwise a few months later when a bridge keeper near Kilsyth (presumably at Auchinstarry) failed to raise the bridge in time and the boat crashed into it. The *Glasgow Courier* of 4 June 1811 reported that the impact 'beat down all the iron railing, carried away part of the helm, stove in the deck, broke the windows, and otherwise materially damaged the boat'. It speculated that there would have been fatalities 'had not the few passengers on the deck time to escape', but sadly for history did not say how.

Passengers had to be wary of their time, because Glasgow and Falkirk clocks were set to different times and a passenger using Glasgow time—taken from St George's Church—could arrive fifteen minutes late for a boat leaving Falkirk. This sort of disparity was common throughout the country and time was only standardised when railway timetables required trains to meet at the same place at the same time![20]

Although steam had been rejected for canal boats, it was becoming established on other waterways. In 1814 a steamboat service was started between Newhaven (Leith) and Grangemouth. Passengers from Glasgow wanting to make the connection had to make their way from Lock 16 to the harbour at the sea lock. A boat operated for a while between Burnhouse (Lock 7) and Grangemouth, but passengers had to walk a mile to catch it and might have been quicker to walk all the way because the boat had to negotiate four locks in two and a half miles. It was superseded by coaches from Lock 16. By 1820 a rival company was competing directly with the canal boats by running coaches all the way from Glasgow to meet the Grangemouth steamer.

Meanwhile the number of people using the passage boats kept on rising and by 1819 was close to the magic figure of 100,000 in a year. In the same year a new passage boat, the *Vulcan*, entered service. She was Scotland's first iron boat, built on the Monkland Canal at Faskine, near Calderbank, where the local ironworks was known for its ability to make malleable iron plate. Doubters, who believed that iron could not float, scoffed at her builder, Thomas Wilson, but he proved them wrong when she was launched on 14 May—and didn't sink! This pioneering vessel weighed just under thirteen tons, was 65 feet long, had a beam of twelve feet, six inches and drew 21 inches of water. She carried passengers for a few years and was then converted for other uses, remaining on the canal for over 60 years. Thomas Wilson went on to take charge of the Canal Company's depot at Tophill in Falkirk where he built more iron boats.[21]

The canal was embracing new ideas, trade was expanding and the start of construction on the Union Canal between Falkirk and Edinburgh brought the promise of a major new market.

Document 1 (Receipt)

No 268

£5

Edinburgh & Glasgow Union Canal Office

1..1 Sh. Edinburgh 9th Aug 1822

We the subscribers, being a quorum of the Committee of Management, do hereby acknowledge the Edin.r and Glasgow Union Canal Company, to have received from Mr John Jeffrey the sum of Five pounds Sterg. which he has this day paid into the Bank of Scotland, on account of the said Union Canal Company, which sum, is the amount of the 10th Call of 10 P. Cent, on 1 Share of the Company's Stock Subscribed by him and which became due on the 11th Nov. 1820 11 May 1822

A Munro

W.m Maxwell

E. Alexander

Entered to Credit of the Edin.r & Glasgow Union Canal Company —

Henry Goodsir Teller

Document 2 (Certificate)

EDINBURGH & GLASGOW
Union Canal Company.

No. 173 a/

In terms of the Act of Parliament establishing the EDINBURGH & GLASGOW UNION CANAL COMPANY, (57 Georgii III. cap. 56, § 30,) These are to certify, That Rodger Aytoun, Banker Greenock is a proprietor of — Five — Shares of the CAPITAL STOCK of the said Canal Company, each Share being Fifty Pounds Sterling; and that these Shares being regularly entered in the Company's Books, he the said Rodger Aytoun Esq.r — is entitled to all the profits and advantages which may arise from the same, and is subject to the same calls, rules, and restrictions which the other proprietors are or may be subject to; as witness my hand this Twenty ninth day of October in the year Eighteen hundred and twenty four.

R. Downie   Chairman.

Edinburgh
Union Canal Office,
Sealed & countersigned by me,
clerk to the Canal Co.

Alex. Cheyne

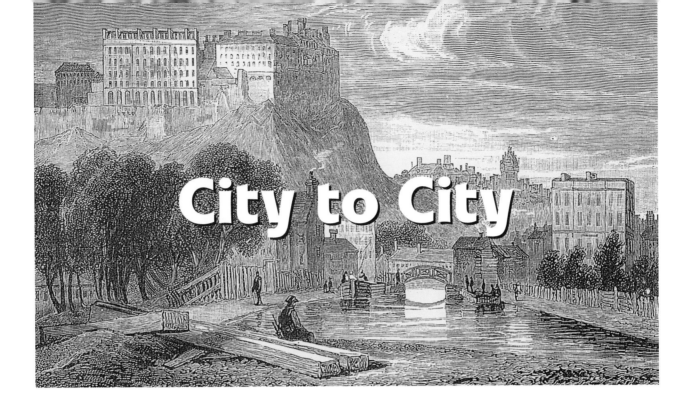

City to City

Port Hopetoun.
City of Glasgow Libraries and Archives; The Mitchell Library.

Edinburgh sits on the northern edge of one of Scotland's richest coalfields, and large quantities of coal could also be delivered by sea from Alloa, Fife and Newcastle. Despite these advantages the principal reason for making the Union Canal was to get coal into the city from the west. The reason was cost. Tax on the ship-borne coal made it very expensive, and local supplies were controlled by a small group of mine owners who operated a price-fixing cartel to keep prices high. Added to that, carters, when they were sober enough to get coal to the city, were adept at cheating their customers by giving short measure. The capital was therefore being held back by a corrupt and costly coal trade while Glasgow was growing fast thanks to cheap and plentiful fuel coming through the Monkland and Forth & Clyde Canals.

Edinburgh's desire to throw off its shackles was shared in Glasgow where a canal between the cities was seen as a way of expanding trade and opening up a new market to Monklands coal. In 1793 the great and good of both places subscribed to a survey from engineers John Ainslie and Robert Whitworth Jnr. They looked at a number of options to connect Leith to the Clyde by way of Shotts and the Monklands coalfield. The mineral resources along the four routes were evaluated by other experts and four years later John Rennie, a Scottish engineer with extensive canal-building experience in England, inspected the routes. He designed another, to the north, which went by Linlithgow, Falkirk and Cumbernauld, before cutting down through the Monklands. Support was split between this route and one of the Whitworth/Ainslie lines. Rennie's route was likely to earn higher passenger revenues, although even he had to concede that the rival route would have greater access to coal reserves. It would, however, have to climb very high to reach them at a cost which deterred investors, and the project lapsed when money became scarce during the Napoleonic wars.

War was still grinding on when the harsh winter of 1813 brought Edinburgh's old problems to the surface. A new survey was done by Hugh

Slateford Aqueduct with the later railway viaduct beyond.

Avon Aqueduct.

Almond Aqueduct: the water falling from the canal is being let out through a sluice on the side of the aqueduct to control the level. There are similar sluices on the other aqueducts and simple spillways over cobbled sections of towpath to allow excess water to overflow into adjacent watercourses.

Baird, who proposed a branch canal from the Forth & Clyde at Falkirk to a terminal in the city's Fountainbridge area. Some people smelled a rat, fearing that because Baird was resident engineer on the Forth & Clyde Canal, that company would benefit from his scheme by sucking trade away from Leith to Grangemouth. A furious war of words broke out. Rennie's route was resurrected as an alternative and another route was surveyed by Robert Stevenson. It ran on one level from Edinburgh to Lock 20 on the Forth & Clyde and included provision for locks to Leith, and from Port Dundas to the Clyde.

Baird's canal had one big advantage—it was cheap. It was also given the ultimate accolade for the time when the great Thomas Telford inspected the route and declared it to be 'the most perfect inland navigation between Edinburgh and Glasgow'.[1] It was planned to run for 31 miles and 163 yards from Edinburgh to Falkirk, be 240 feet above sea level, five feet deep, 40 feet wide at the top and twenty at the bottom. A prospectus was published, full of optimistic phrases like 'it is impossible that it can fail' and '[when joined to the Forth & Clyde it will] find a ready trade waiting for it'. Attracted by such confidence and estimated costs of £235,000, offset by earnings of £52,000 a year, investors backed the project. Opponents lobbied hard to the end, but the canal was approved by Parliament in June 1817.

Plans for the first blocks of work were drawn up and newspaper advertisements invited people to inspect them at the company's Edinburgh offices. By February 1818 contractors had been appointed and on 3 March the committee of management adjourned their general meeting and proceeded to where the new terminal basin, Port Hopetoun, would be formed. It was in an area of open parks and town houses, one of which—belonging to the Earl of Hopetoun—was adjacent to the proposed basin. The engineer and contractor were waiting on the site when the committee arrived. Company chairman Robert Downie of Appin made a short speech which ended 'I will now convince you, gentlemen [presumably no ladies were present!], that some of your committee can handle a spade as well as a pen'. Then he cut a square of turf and, as he threw it into the air, the crowd cheered. The minister of St Cuthbert's Parish, the Revd Dr David Dickson, blessed the project and received a ten guinea donation from the company for the poor of the parish. The contractor also received five guineas so that the workmen could drink to the canal's success— free drink no doubt gave them a warm feeling for the job![2]

The canal sparked an upsurge in economic activity, with suppliers placing notices in the papers offering wood, iron, wagons, barrows, machinery and tools. These coincided with the company inviting offers for contracts for the central section of canal from the Rivers Almond to Avon. But as work got under way, proposals were being aired in Edinburgh for a railway to go east to the coalfields of East Lothian. The arguments over the canal's route had taken so long that future problems were already looming.[3]

The Union was one of the last canals to be made in Britain. Its sophisticated engineering represented the pinnacle of the canal-builder's art, but it also pointed the way for railway construction by using embankments, cuttings, a tunnel, culverts, bridges and great multi-arched aqueducts to maintain a level track.

The Aqueducts

The aqueducts over the Rivers Avon and Almond, and the Water of Leith at Slateford, were arguably the finest of their kind in Britain. They were made

Laughin' and Greetin' Bridge

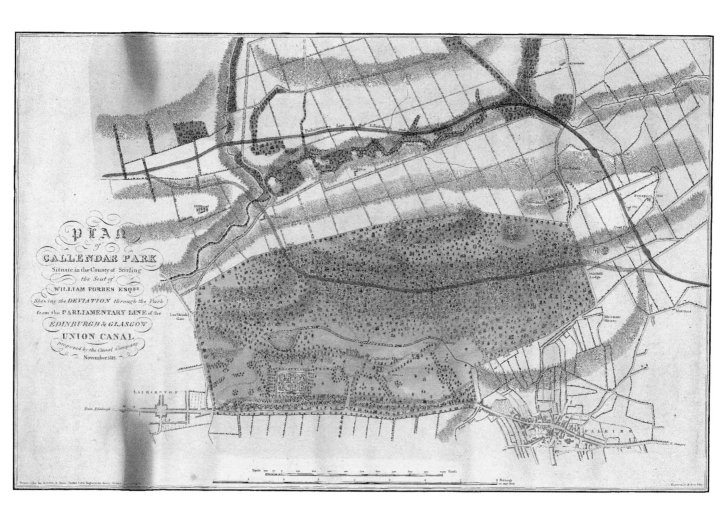

with hollow, internally buttressed masonry piers set 50 feet apart and spanned by arches carrying a stone-clad iron trough. The use of such troughs to contain the water meant that the rest of the structures could be kept to a refined elegance unobtainable in the all stone aqueducts of the Forth & Clyde. The plates for the iron troughs were made in Shrewsbury.

Slateford Aqueduct became an object of wonder and a journalist inspected its construction in June 1820. (His report in the *Glasgow Courier* may have appeared elsewhere because newspapers at the time often reprinted their rivals' articles verbatim.) He walked along the iron trough and wrote of it: 'The cast iron frame over the arches, through which the canal is to pass, is nearly completed and resembles the hull of a vessel of extraordinary length. The sides are formed of large concave cast iron plates, and the flooring, or bed, is composed of the same material; these are bolted together and the seams caulked'. He thought it a 'stupendous undertaking' and considered that the finished structure would 'add greatly to the romantic scenery of the place'. The people of Inglis Green thought otherwise because the great structure overshadowed their bleachfield![4]

Slateford Aqueduct had eight arches, was 600 feet long and 65 feet high. The Almond, with its five arches, was 420 feet long and 76 feet high. But the 85 foot high, twelve arch Avon was the crowning glory. At 810 feet it was the second longest canal aqueduct in Britain.

Water

The principal water supply entered the canal beside the Almond Aqueduct. The water was taken from the Almond about three miles upstream of the aqueduct and the feeder lade ran along the river's west side for a short distance before crossing to the east bank on a neat cast iron aqueduct. From there it ran down the valley, like a miniature canal, over culverts, under bridges and through four little tunnels. It was an extraordinary piece of engineering.

The canal's use of the river alarmed mill owners who depended upon its water for power, so the Canal Company also created the huge Cobbinshaw Reservoir high in the hills above West Calder. Water from it, flowing down the Bog Burn and into the river, was used to compensate the Almond's flow, particularly in dry seasons. The reservoir came very close to running dry in 1824 and so the company looked seriously at creating a feeder from the Avon. They even thought about making it navigable up to Carribber Mill, but the idea was not carried through and the Almond feeder remained the principal supply.

The Falkirk Tunnel

The canal's route was fixed by an Act of Parliament which also contained specific restrictions on the use of private property. The most awkward location was Callendar House at Falkirk where landowner William Forbes had refused to allow the canal to pass through his grounds. The only alternative was to make a tunnel under Prospect Hill, but before work began there, and at some other places, the company tried to persuade Parliament to allow them to alter the route. They met stern opposition. Forbes had died in 1815 and the estate was being administered on behalf of his young son by trustees who refused to budge from the father's position. Parliament rejected the company's proposal to go through the estate to the north of the hill, and the tunnel had to be cut.

It would be the third in Scotland, as two tunnels had existed since 1811 on the Glasgow, Paisley & Ardrossan Canal, one of 70 yards at Ralston Square and the other, of 80 yards, at Causewayside. Another 80 yard tunnel was made

Map showing the line of the canal through the Callendar Estate which the company hoped would avoid their having to excavate the tunnel.
Bob McCutcheon.

Tunnel at Ralston Square on the Glasgow, Paisley & Ardrossan Canal.

The Falkirk tunnel's eastern portal.

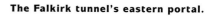

The Falkirk locks.

Inside the Falkirk tunnel.

in the 1840s on the branch canal which connected Langloan Ironworks to the Monkland main line. So the Union Canal's tunnel was not the only one in the country, but it was by far the most spectacular. It was cut through solid rock for 696 yards by men working in from both ends, and in both directions from the bases of shafts driven into the intended line from above.

The plan was to create a thirteen foot wide waterway with a five foot wide tracking path. The roof was to be twelve feet above top bank level, although the additional requirement that if it was unstable at this level it should be taken up to where it would stand safely on its own resulted in a wide, cavernous interior. Only where roof material was loose, and where a geological intrusion occurred about halfway through, were masonry arches introduced, although some arching was not completed until after the canal had been opened for a couple of years. The entrances were each finished with arched, dressed masonry and lined for a short distance. Hammer-dressed rubble masonry was used to build up the tracking path where the rock was unstable.[5]

The canal's route across large estates meant that it was always going to be vulnerable to landowners making costly demands or seeking premium rates for ground. The company resorted to the courts on a number of occasions and, after their bruising with the tunnel, had a pyrrhic victory over William Forbes' estate in July 1820. The dispute was over the price of freestone from a quarry on Falkirk Muir. The jury at the Sheriff Court ruled that the company had offered more than twice what the stone was worth and so the Forbes' estate had to sell the stone for less and pay costs![6]

A mile west of the tunnel was the flight of eleven locks that took the canal down to join the Forth & Clyde, a total fall of 112 feet, nine inches. The locks were 69 feet long, twelve feet six inches wide, with a fall of ten feet three inches. They were built by the Falkirk contractor James Wyse, whose inscription for repair work appears on some Forth & Clyde locks. At the foot of the locks was the large junction basin between the two canals. It was called Port Downie, after Robert Downie of Appin.

Navvies

Canals were known as navigations and the tough men (and some women disguised as men) who built them were called navigators—or navvies for short. They were an itinerant workforce that moved around the country from job to job. Some on the Union Canal were English; many, if not most, were Irish. There were numerous Highlanders too, although their tendency to go home at harvest time made contractors wary of employing them. Local people also worked on the construction although a contemporary description of the Falkirk tunnel suggested that Scots could not 'stand the work' and it was done by Irish labourers who were 'a bad set'![7]

The sudden arrival of large numbers of these hard-living, hard-drinking characters must have shocked the douce inhabitants of towns and villages along the route. But the locals were not the only people who were unhappy with their new neighbours; some groups of navvies did not get on with each other either and simply added fighting and feuding to an already uncomfortable and often dangerous life.

Unlike their modern counterparts, they had no health and safety law to protect them and many suffered the consequences. The contractor for the Winchburgh section had to deal with an outbreak of fever amongst his workforce and made arrangements for the men to be admitted to the infirmary in

Clifton Hall Bridge spans the cutting where the woolly mammoth tusk was found.

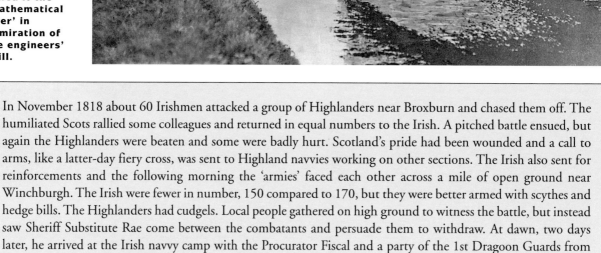

A canal such as the Union, winding on one level over embankments and through cuttings for most of its length, is properly known as a contour canal, although some folk called it the 'mathematical river' in admiration of the engineers' skill.

In November 1818 about 60 Irishmen attacked a group of Highlanders near Broxburn and chased them off. The humiliated Scots rallied some colleagues and returned in equal numbers to the Irish. A pitched battle ensued, but again the Highlanders were beaten and some were badly hurt. Scotland's pride had been wounded and a call to arms, like a latter-day fiery cross, was sent to Highland navvies working on other sections. The Irish also sent for reinforcements and the following morning the 'armies' faced each other across a mile of open ground near Winchburgh. The Irish were fewer in number, 150 compared to 170, but they were better armed with scythes and hedge bills. The Highlanders had cudgels. Local people gathered on high ground to witness the battle, but instead saw Sheriff Substitute Rae come between the combatants and persuade them to withdraw. At dawn, two days later, he arrived at the Irish navvy camp with the Procurator Fiscal and a party of the 1st Dragoon Guards from Stirling. Five men were arrested and taken to the county jail; others absconded. The dragoons took up station at Linlithgow, which no doubt pleased local people fearful of the rowdy, unwelcome strangers in their midst.[8]

The contractor whose employees had engaged in this affray had conveniently gone to Glasgow on business, despite having heard the sound of bagpipes passing his house the night before. He put the source of the trouble down to jealousy and an unlicensed house at Niddry which served drink at all hours of the day and night, including Sundays.

Edinburgh. In response the company agreed to subscribe to the infirmary so that future admissions would be easier, but that did not stop accidents. In October 1819 a young man working near Linlithgow was injured when a sandbank gave way. The surgeons on the spot decided to amputate his leg, but apparently failed to notice that broken ribs had punctured his lungs, and he died a few hours later. They should have known better; another man had died in a similar accident a month earlier. In September 1820 a man was buried when banking at Slateford collapsed. He was dug out quickly but died within hours. Many navvying colleagues attended his funeral.[10]

While digging to the west of Ratho in the summer of 1820, some navvies unearthed the tusk of a woolly mammoth 25 feet down in the clay soil. Sir Alexander Maitland of Clifton Hall, on whose land it was discovered, declined to take charge of it until it was decided if he, or the Canal Company, owned it. Such gentlemanly niceties were too much for the navvies who simply took the tusk to Edinburgh and sold it, as ivory, to a toy maker on the South Bridge. Sir Alexander was not pleased. He tracked the tusk down and bought it back, although a few inches had been cut from it and it was in three pieces. It was displayed for some years at Clifton Hall, and after going missing for a while a piece was found and deposited in the Museum of Scotland.[11]

The realisation that some navvies intended to stay when the canal was finished horrified local communities, but by the 1840s Ratho appeared to have recovered from the shock. In his account of the parish for the *New Statistical Account* the minister wrote that 'time has produced a marked change for the better . . . those [families] that remain have come under the humanising influence of good neighbourhood and Protestant institutions'. He did however yield to the temptation of railing against the 'crying evil' of intemperance and conceded that the Scottish population, like the Irish, needed to improve!

Two former Irish navvies, William Burke and William Hare, achieved fame of a kind. Hare worked on the canal in the Edinburgh area and after it opened was employed as a docker. Burke worked as a navvy near Maddiston and later as a lengthsman (someone who maintained a length of canal) in Edinburgh. When Hare moved into lodgings at Tanner's Close, in the city's West Port area, he soon irritated the landlord, another former canal navvy, by paying too much attention to his wife, who had also worked as a navvy disguised as a man. Hare was kicked out, but when the landlord died soon after he moved back in and took over both wife and lodgings.

At the time the anatomy school in Edinburgh needed fresh corpses for its lessons and did deals with 'resurrection men', or 'body snatchers', who raided graveyards for newly buried bodies. Burke and Hare are usually thought of as grave robbers, but the bodies they supplied never got near a burial. The first was that of an old woman who died at the West Port lodgings. It was a stroke of luck, but the sale of her body inspired the villains to obtain more corpses, and when people failed conveniently to die for them they were murdered.

The Opening

1821 began with confident predictions that the canal would be opened in August, but when it wasn't newspapers published conflicting stories about probable completion dates. Some thought the following spring was most likely, others confidently asserted that—because contractors would pay heavy penalties if they failed to finish by 1 October—that would be the date. By November, with the onset of winter weather and short, dark days, even the optimists thought

A description of a navvy encampment appeared in the *Edinburgh Evening Courant* in December 1822. Alas it is not clear if the people were still working on the canal or unemployed with nowhere to go; destitute strangers in a land that regarded them with suspicion and contempt.

Along the banks of the Union Canal certain edifices have been erected which strike the traveller with no little astonishment. These are erected by Irish labourers upon some few vacant spots of ground belonging to the canal proprietors, and are pointed out to strangers in the passage boats as great curiosities. Each of course is more wretched than another and presents a picture of squalid poverty which is new to the people on this side of the channel. One of them, with the exception perhaps of a few sticks, is composed entirely of rotten straw; its dimensions would not suffice for a pig-sty, and its form is that of a beehive, only it is more conical. The smoke which does not escape at the door penetrates through every part of the structure, which thus presents the appearance of a hay-rick on fire. A Hottentot kraal, in comparison with it, is a palace. In the midst of so much misery, the children appear healthful and frolicsome, and the men and women contented and happy.[9]

The Union Canal's bridges were built to a fixed headroom and numbered, excluding the drawbridges, 1-62 from east to west. Most conform to a standard pattern, as at Learielaw Bridge (opposite top), but there are differences in size and parapet design and some, like Craigton Bridge, with its octagonal pillars and monogrammed keystones, are more decorative.

the canal was unlikely to open until March, four years after the start of construction. It was still a huge achievement for a time when the sweat and blood of manual labour did what machines do now, and it was unfortunate that it was marred by unmet predictions of early completion.[12]

The Canal Company set up a boat-building yard at Gilmore Place, near Lochrin Distillery, to build 'elegant and comfortable' passage boats. The first, *Flora MacIvor*, was launched on Hogmanay 1821. Preparations began by candlelight before one o'clock in the morning, but as the day broke the men were still hard at work. They continued past midday and many people who had come to watch drifted away, but at four o'clock in the afternoon everything was ready. The blocks were removed, the boat slid towards the water, but stopped before reaching it. Ropes were attached and she was finally dragged into the basin at twenty minutes to five. The crowd, or what was left of it, cheered![13]

Crowds converged on the canal again three weeks later when rumours of a company inspection spread through the country. It was obvious that something was going to happen because work had been stepped up prior to the event and was even being done through the night by the light of flaming torches. When the committee of management, on board the *Flora MacIvor*, sailed into Linlithgowshire (West Lothian) and then Stirlingshire they were greeted by bands, bonfires and cheering, flag-waving crowds. At places the throng stopped the track horses and the boat was hauled along by eager people. On the way, *Flora MacIvor* passed the first two boats bound for Edinburgh with coal from Meadowbank, near Polmont, and committee members donated twenty tons of the cargo to the Destitute Sick Society—it was common practice for well-off people to donate coal to those in need. Progress was halted at the unfinished tunnel, but the committee left the boat and were taken through on the railway used by the contractor to remove spoil. A line of blazing torches lit their way.[14]

The euphoria of this ceremonial journey subsided over the next few months as work on the tunnel continued to delay full opening of the canal. The second passage boat, *Di Vernon*, was launched at Gilmore Place on 2 March. She too had an eventful entry to the water when her stern stuck in the canal bed before the bow was clear of the slip. She was eased afloat without damage. (The names *Flora MacIvor*, *Di* [Diana] *Vernon* and the later *Jeannie Deans* and *Baillie Nicol Jarvie* were those of characters from Walter Scott novels—the latest in popular fiction at the time.)[15]

One morning towards the end of March the two passage boats set off for their first trip to the Avon Aqueduct. On board were subscribers who had plenty to eat and drink and were entertained with music. The outward journey was hampered by low water level, but this was raised during the day making for a speedier return. A similar trip for members of the public was made the following day. Sailings began in early April between Edinburgh and East Shielhill Bridge, although some hold-ups had to be endured before the service could be described as 'regular'.[16]

Anticipation grew in Edinburgh where construction work had been finished for some time and contractors were selling off surplus materials. Favourable rates had been set so that mine owners from the distant Monklands could sell their fuel profitably in the capital and people could sense that the long wait for cheap coal from 'inexhaustible supplies' was nearly over. In early May it was reported that the canal was in water from end to end and a few days later a boat loaded with flagstones from Denny Quarry sailed into Edinburgh: the canal was open. There was no ceremony, it was just open![17]

Stamp used at Port Hopetoun to verify the origin of coal.

Drawbridge No. 3, Gilmore Park   Crown Copyright: Royal Commission on the Ancient and Historical Monuments of Scotland (Chrystal Collection).

blether at the bridge

The first four bridges west of Port Hopetoun: Semple Street, Fountainbridge, Gilmore Park and Viewforth were 'drawbridges'—single leaf bascule bridges. They were manned by keepers who appear to have indulged in extramural activities. At bridge No. 1, at Semple Street, the keeper also ran a public house while the man at No. 3 kept cows and pigs.

Traffic and Trade

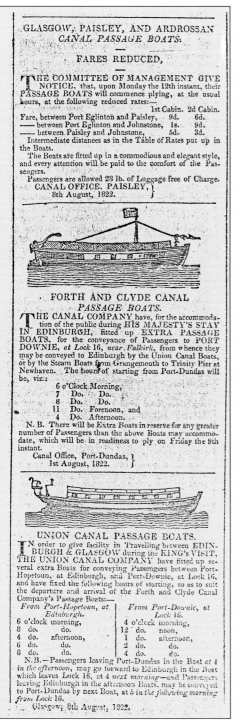

Coal prices across the city started to fall as soon as the canal opened. Merchants set up depots at Port Hopetoun and one pair whose names—Burke and Henry—were uncannily similar to the port's other entrepreneurs, equipped themselves with four boats and shipped in coal from Parkhall Colliery at Falkirk. They operated their own carts, but other merchants made use of the city's carters, a notorious band of rogues who were adept at 'losing' coal between the depot and delivery. One man, not connected with the canal, was found, twice in ten days, trying to pass off seventeen hundredweight or less as a ton (twenty hundredweight). The Canal Company installed weighing machines and issued tickets which carters had to present to customers in an attempt to cut out fraud. Anyone suspecting short measure was advised to send the cart back to Port Hopetoun to be reweighed. The ticket also let people know that the coal had come from the canal and not another source.[18]

Despite these efforts, the public's distrust of the industry was so deep-seated that it took time to persuade them to buy coal from the canal. The practice of the time was for people to buy coal in large lumps known as 'great coal'. They did this so that they could see what they were getting, but coal loaded in and out of boats inevitably broke into small lumps and so potential customers were reluctant to buy for fear of being cheated with an uncertain mixture. Despite these difficulties, coal from a variety of sources, including the Monklands, Falkirk and Clackmannanshire started to reach Port Hopetoun. Two years later the volume coming into the city was such that a second basin was made specially for the coal trade. It was called Port Hamilton, in recognition of the Duke of Hamilton's great efforts to supply the city with coal from his estate at Redding. Coal merchants were encouraged to move from the old basin to the new, although they had to bid at a roup for the best sites.

Rules were laid down for boat operators. Skippers had to secure cargoes properly and ensure that nothing fell in the canal when loading and unloading. If anything was thrown overboard the culprit would be fined, while leaky boats would be banned and open boats had to have adequate freeboard to prevent being swamped. The skipper of a trading boat faced a heavy fine if he failed to give way to a passage boat. He had to provide himself with a horn and blow it on approaching bridges and aqueducts, and he had to stay off an aqueduct if another boat, travelling in the opposite direction, was already on it. A strict order of precedence was established should a dispute arise. Use of the locks was regulated to preserve water and lights had to be shown at night. Landing on the offside was prohibited, except in an emergency. No one under fifteen years of age was allowed to navigate or track a boat and any tracker found on a boat and not with his horse during passage would be fined and could lose his license.[19]

The Union's early passage boats were large, solid vessels. They left Port Hopetoun at 7 a.m. and 4 p.m. and, despite having an unimpeded track, took seven hours to get to the head of the locks at Falkirk.

The journey may not have been quick, but in August 1822 King George IV visited Edinburgh and the frequency of passage boats was more than doubled for the three weeks of his stay. Hundreds of people travelled to see him, many of them carried on ordinary barges with planks of wood as makeshift seats. The sight of the portly king in a too-short kilt and flesh-coloured tights did little to enhance the image of the monarchy, but the visit was a bonanza for the two canals.[20]

When the excitement was over the passage boats settled into a routine.

Bill for the luggage boat *Appin*, named after the estate of Union Canal chairman Robert Downie.

One arrived at Port Hopetoun on a dark November night in 1822 with members of the Edinburgh Theatre Company on board. They had been appearing in Glasgow and had a lot of luggage which was being arranged on a truck when a man missed his footing and fell into the water. As he was pulled out, another theatre man fell in. He too was rescued, minus his umbrella, just as Mrs Nicol, a popular entertainer, went in. Her voluminous clothes kept her afloat long enough for her to grab a boathook and be hauled to safety. It sounds like a farce and it was certainly dramatic, but this comedy of errors was also excellent publicity at the start of the new season! Mrs Nicol was on stage at the Theatre Royal a few days later, none the worse for what the *Edinburgh Evening Courant* described as her 'aquatic excursion'.[21]

The passage boats' routine was interrupted a few times by breaches to the canal banks. There were two near Hermiston, the second of which, in December 1822, was serious and stopped the boats. Passengers were taken around it by road: coaches took those from cabin class while steerage travellers went in carts. Ice blocked the canal in January 1823 and an attempt to break a passage through it was abandoned because of fears that the action of putting pressure on the ice could breach the banks. Leaks and breaches were already a feature of the Union Canal before its first year was out and they continued to cause problems thereafter.[22]

At Falkirk, the passage boats terminated above the locks and passengers had to walk down to Lock 16 on the Forth & Clyde Canal to catch the boat to Glasgow. A local operator was allowed to run a coach service for passengers and a cart for their luggage, but in 1823 the canal was extended by 560 yards to a new terminal, Port Maxwell, which shortened the distance people had to walk. The following year, when a water shortage threatened to close the canal, plans were made to stop luggage boats from using the locks and to have their cargoes transferred by cart from Port Maxwell to the Forth & Clyde, but the rains came and the measures were never implemented.

The luggage boats were operated by a private company, the London, Leith, Edinburgh & Glasgow Shipping Company. They travelled at night and from 1824 were allowed to carry steerage passengers. Another company, the Edinburgh and Glasgow Canal Shipping Company, which was contracted to the Forth & Clyde Canal Company, also started operating night luggage and cargo boats. At Port Hopetoun, a large warehouse was built for the luggage boats on the square jetty which projected into the basin, but the passage boats were also expected to use the jetty and in 1824 Robert Downie was annoyed to discover they were not doing so. A broad stage with a roof was erected for them and they were instructed not to berth anywhere else!

Day-to-day management had taken over from the frenetic construction phase, but the canal had cost almost double what had been predicted while revenues were only a third. Finances were in a bad way and any hopes of long-term improvement were about to be dashed.

NEW DAILY CONVEYANCE
FOR GOODS
BETWEEN EDINBURGH AND GLASGOW.

IN consequence of new arrangements made by the FORTH and CLYDE and UNION CANAL COMPANIES, the LONDON, LEITH, EDINBURGH, and GLASGOW SHIPPING CO. have been induced to put such a number of BOATS on these CANALS as will ensure a regular daily conveyance for GOODS between EDINBURGH and GLASGOW, and after the 15th instant, a Boat will leave Port Hopetoun and Port-Dundas every afternoon at Four o'clock, by which all the dispatch of Land Carriage will be obtained, while the charges will generally be 30 per cent. lower.

Goods sent by this conveyance for places beyond Edinburgh, will be regularly delivered to the respective Carriers without any additional charge.

Agents, { WILLIAM CRICHTON, 60, Queen Street, Glasgow.
JOHN STRACHAN, Port Hopetoun, Edinburgh.

The terminal of the Garnkirk & Glasgow Railway beside the canal at St Rollox.

Bob McCutcheon.

Viewforth Bridge

blether at the bridge

Viewforth Bridge, originally drawbridge No. 4, had been rebuilt in stone by the 1840s and is unnumbered, although just to confuse the unwary the keystones appear to show a number one—not all things written on tablets of stone can be believed! Above them are carved stones with the castle from Edinburgh's coat of arms on the east side and Glasgow's heraldic tree on the west.

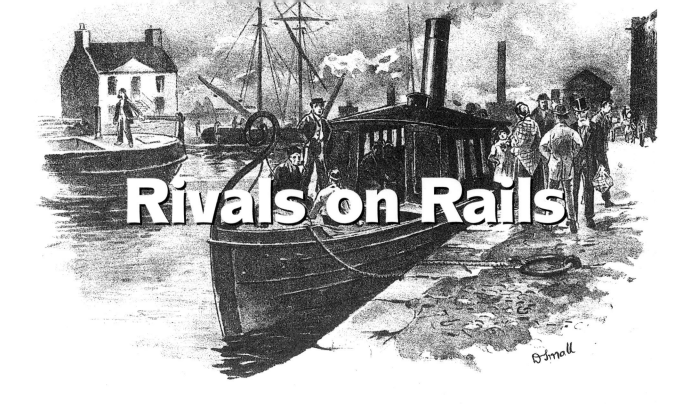

Rivals on Rails

Rockvilla Castle: drawing by David Small.

City of Glasgow Libraries and Archives; The Mitchell Library.

Rails were used to benefit canals long before they became a threat. Horse-drawn railways, or inclines worked by gravity, were built to bring the products of mines and quarries to canals for onward shipment. One of the best examples was at Muirkirk in Ayrshire where minerals, let down hillsides in trucks, were loaded onto barges for a two-mile canal journey to the local ironworks.

Other early mineral railways were likewise developed in association with water transport. The Tranent wagonway in East Lothian, over which the Battle of Prestonpans was fought in 1745, took coal to Cockenzie Harbour. A railway linked the Fordell mines in Fife to the new St David's Harbour on the Forth and another line went from the Devon mines to Alloa Harbour. But while these simple railways might have lulled some canal proprietors into believing that water transport would always remain supreme, others thought differently.[1]

A plan to build a railway to bring Midlothian coal into Edinburgh spurred the Union Canal proprietors into devising a scheme of their own to counter the threat. They proposed a line to run more or less on the route of the present M8 motorway from Polkemmet and Whitburn to the canal at Ryal near Broxburn. Branches to it from Houston and Bathgate were also considered and the Parliamentary bill authorising construction was passed in 1825, although the railway was never made.

Ironically, completion of the Union Canal and the opening up of a huge new market for Monklands coal triggered Scotland's rail revolution. Barges bound for Edinburgh first had to go into Glasgow on the Monkland Canal and then back out on the Forth & Clyde. This cost time and money and traders quickly concluded that a railway to Kirkintilloch, only ten miles north of the coalfield, would speed things up. Construction of the Monkland & Kirkintilloch Railway began in 1824 and it was completed in 1826. It snaked along, linking up numerous collieries before heading for the canal. Trains were initially horse-hauled, but steam locomotives were introduced in 1831 making it the first

Railway wagon boat.

Prospectus for the proposed Stirling Canal.

Bowling Harbour c.1905.

CANAL PASSENGER BOAT.

187 Trongate, Glasgow

PROSPECTUS
OF
A CANAL,
Intended to connect the Town of
STIRLING
WITH
THE CITIES OF
EDINBURGH & GLASGOW,
and the Towns of
PAISLEY, GREENOCK,
AND
PORT GLASGOW.

Canal Night Passenger & Goods Boat.

steam-hauled public railway in Scotland. Initially it terminated at a canalside wharf, but soon a large basin was created where coal could be stored and boats loaded. This was enlarged in 1841.

In the mid-1830s a boat was fitted with rails and turntables. The idea was that wagons of coal could be loaded directly onto it at Kirkintilloch and taken to Grangemouth where they would be run off and the contents loaded onto coal boats. It cut out double-handling and, by protecting the coal from being broken into smaller lumps, kept the price high. It is believed to be the first example of a rail-ferry in the world.

The Monkland & Kirkintilloch became the core of a network, with other railways forming junctions with it. The most significant was at Gartsherrie from where the Garnkirk & Glasgow Railway ran in an arc north of the Monkland Canal. It opened in 1831 to a terminal beside the shallow Cut of Junction at St Rollox, Glasgow. This was not a link to the canal, but an independent railway competing directly with it. The threat had begun to take shape, although in this case the coal and iron industries generated so much trade that both canal and railway thrived for many years.

Roads were also causing concern. On short routes like Glasgow to Kirkintilloch, vans and carts began to take traffic away from the canal and, with more coaches available, people could choose how they travelled. Commercial carriers also had a choice and the Forth & Clyde Canal Company responded by reducing rates on certain commodities to encourage companies not to send their goods overland. Road improvements also started to disrupt canal operations. In 1831 the canal below Lock 16 was closed to allow the aqueduct at Camelon to be replaced by a bridge, while at the same time the road through Grangemouth was realigned across the canal at Lock 2 and over the embankment for the timber basins.

Despite the growing competition, people still saw a future in canals. The Forth & Clyde Company thought about making a branch canal from either Wyndford Lock or Castlecary to Dennyloanhead and another group published a prospectus in 1835 for a canal all the way to Stirling. Another branch canal was proposed the following year, to run from Glasgow Road Bridge, a mile west of Kirkintilloch, to the Hurlet and Campsie Alum Works at Lennoxtown.

The Forth & Cart Junction Canal at Whitecrook.
West Dunbartonshire Libraries; Clydebank Library.

None of these were made, but work did start in 1838 on a half-mile long canal intended to give access to Paisley from the Forth & Clyde. Known as the Forth & Cart Junction Canal, or any abbreviation contemporary scribes chose to use, it had three locks and two bridges, and ran straight from Whitecrook to the Clyde opposite the River Cart. It was opened when an official barge sailed from Port Dundas to Paisley in May 1840. Coal boats did use the little canal, but it was never a great success and was abandoned in 1893.[2]

At Bowling, a new outer harbour was made in the late 1840s and a new sea lock built to give access to it from an extended canal basin. The new lock was sheltered by the harbour and superseded the old sea lock which had always been difficult to go in and out of.[3]

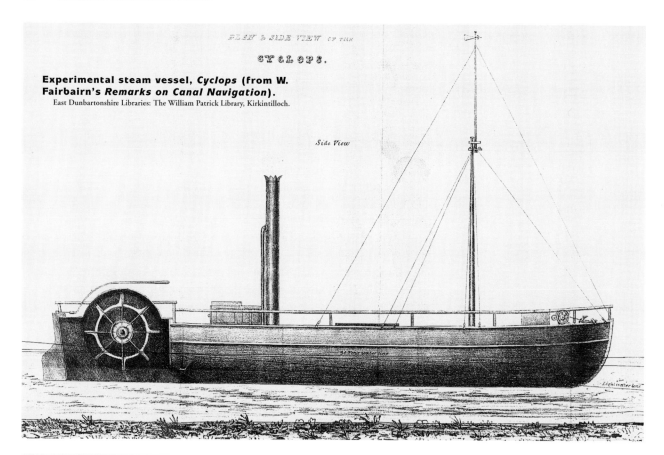

Experimental steam vessel, *Cyclops* (from W. Fairbairn's *Remarks on Canal Navigation*).
East Dunbartonshire Libraries: The William Patrick Library, Kirkintilloch.

***Sunbeam*, the last light-iron passage boat to operate on the Glasgow, Paisley & Ardrossan Canal.**

Swifts

By the late 1820s the canal companies realised they would have to develop faster boats to retain passenger traffic. In the thinking of the time, fast meant vessels with a narrow beam and the Forth & Clyde Canal Company conducted trials with a new boat called *Cyclops*. She was not a great success, but council member Thomas Grahame used the experience to persuade his colleagues to look again at using steam. In 1828 a small Clyde paddle steamer, *Cupid*, was tried as a tug and showed that the fear of damage to the canal banks and puddle-clay lining, which had coloured thinking since the *Charlotte Dundas*, was unfounded. Now in favour of steam, the company had *Cyclops*'s hull widened and a steam engine and stern paddle wheel fitted. They experimented with her as a tug and she was later used to carry goods and passengers between Port Dundas and Alloa.

Speeding up the passenger boats was still the priority and for inspiration the two canal companies looked south of the Clyde to the Glasgow, Paisley & Ardrossan Canal. Despite its name this canal ran from Port Eglinton, Glasgow, to a terminal at Johnstone. The eight mile stretch between Paisley and the city was a commuter canal for which fast, light iron boats, 70 feet long by eight feet beam, had been developed. They carried 60 to 70 passengers with no luggage, and were whisked along the lock-free canal by two horses at an average speed of nine miles an hour.

Operating such boats on the Forth & Clyde Canal would not be so simple. The locks would slow them down and limit their size, and the tow line would have to be dropped at bridges, but Thomas Grahame was not put off. He began to experiment with two narrow-beam boats tied together as a single twin-hulled vessel and in 1830 had such a boat specially built. She was called *Swift* and was tried out between Port Dundas and Port Hopetoun. The outward journey took seven and a quarter hours, but the return run to the west was completed half an hour faster, with three horses towing for part of the time. A steam engine was installed in an attempt to speed her up, but that was unsuccessful and so she carried on, horse-hauled, until halted by ice. She did not resume in the spring because the Union Canal Company were unwilling to sanction daytime services between the cities.

Swift's wooden hulls made her vulnerable, so she did not last long on other services, but her name lived on with all the fast boats that followed being popularly known as swifts. The hull design was also used as the basis for the *Lord Dundas*, a stern paddle steamer that was built in Manchester and sailed up to the canal in 1831. The following year the same builder produced another steamer, the *Manchester*, based on the old *Cyclops*—but try as they might, the steamers did not speed up passenger services.

East Dunbartonshire Libraries: The William Patrick Library, Kirkintilloch.

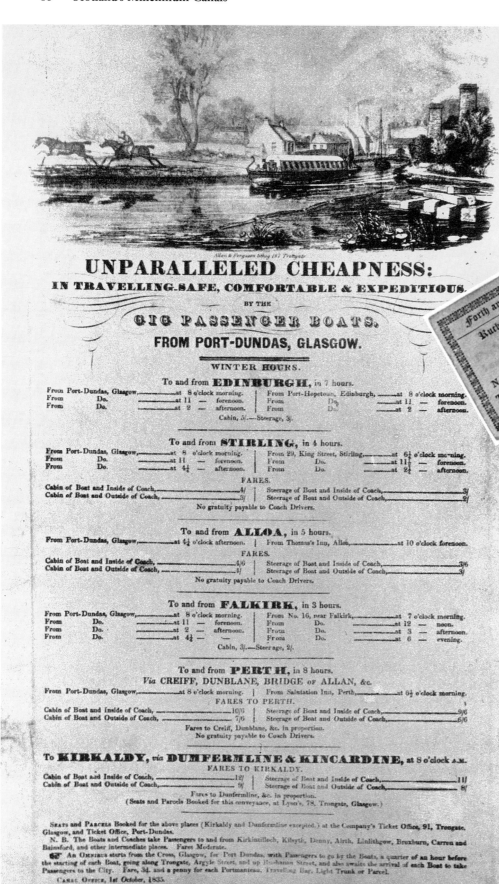

East Dunbartonshire Libraries: The William Patrick Library, Kirkintilloch.

They found a new role in 1832 when cholera broke out in Kirkintilloch. Glasgow and Maryhill were also affected, but Kirkintilloch seemed to worry the authorities most. They suggested unloading boats either side of the town and taking goods around by cart, but that was silly because the road also went through the town! As a compromise they allowed boats to be towed between Glasgow Road Bridge and Inchbelly by *Lord Dundas* and *Cyclops*. The delay and inconvenience at Kirkintilloch was not the only effect of the outbreak. Ships had to wait outside the canal for ten days to comply with quarantine restrictions and, as a result, many avoided it and revenue dropped by twenty per cent on the previous year.

The canal companies still wanted to speed up passenger services and set about developing fast horse-hauled boats. Two, *Rapid* and *Velocity*, were built at Tophill, along with an experimental steamer, the *Edinburgh*. They all entered service in 1833 as night boats operating a through service between Port Hopetoun and Port Dundas. These fast boats, with a light at their bow and the hooting of a horn to warn of their presence, became known as 'hoolets', the Scots word for owls. Three months later the *Edinburgh* hit a bridge on the Union Canal and was withdrawn.

Through the 1830s the companies concentrated on speeding up their boats with improved design and sleek, light iron construction. A succession of boats entered the service until, by the high season of 1835, there were seven a day on the Forth & Clyde. Five of them met connecting boats to Edinburgh and the city to city journey could be made in seven and half hours. Coach connections were also advertised to Stirling, Alloa, Perth, Crieff, Dunblane, Bridge of Allan, Dollar and Kincardine, while in Glasgow an omnibus catered for passengers going between the canal and the Irish steamers at the Broomielaw. A floating bridge was put in across the canal at Stockingfield. It was made by Reid & Hanna of Paisley, who built many of the new fast boats, and helped to speed up journey times by allowing horses to cross the main line to Bowling without having to pass under Lochburn Road Aqueduct.[4]

In a further experiment to speed operations, rails were laid along the towpath near Lock 16 in August 1839 and a steam locomotive was tried as a means of hauling boats. The idea was not taken up because of concerns about expense and towage round bends.[5]

blether at the bridge

In 1834, about 100 years before this camper pitched his tent at Hermiston, the engineer, mathematician and naval architect John Scott Russell was watching trials of a boat near here. He noticed that when it stopped the bow wave kept going and so he followed it on horseback for about two miles before it dissipated on the bends of the canal. He realised that this phenomenon was important, but the real significance of the wave eluded science until many years after his death. Electronic engineers are now trying to harness what is known as the solitary wave, or soliton, as a pulse of light like a bell-like wave for high-speed optical transmission down fibre-optic cables.

Hermiston

Luggage-boat Blues

Not everyone could afford to use the fast boats. A self-styled 'adventurer', who endured a journey on a luggage boat, recalled it many years later:[6]

When I first journeyed from Scotland into England, nearly half the time was spent on the canal boat that crept from Edinburgh to Glasgow. There were two kinds of boat on the canal, the swifter of which was called the 'fly' boat. It went from Edinburgh to Glasgow in about six hours, and was the passenger boat. The other was overloaded with heavy goods of a miscellaneous character; and no one journeyed on it except those who travelled with the goods, and such adventurers as myself, who could not afford to be particular. Everyone, I suppose, has seen the half-barge, half-raft called a canal boat which crawls after its horse on the bank at the rate of a mile an hour.

When we set off it seemed to me that the horse moved but that the boat remained stationary. In the gathering darkness, the rope that connected them was invisible and the horse was but a shadow. On the whole the motion was pleasant enough. I had no watch, but I compared our movement to the hour-hand. Since then I have often travelled on the fly-boat and enjoyed it. The horses raced along with it, keeping up a steady pace of some seven miles an hour. Our horses—they were frequently changed—had probably never tried to trot in their lives. Perhaps they were like the Skye ponies, which accept a lash as a signal to come to a full stop. I stood and sat, hour about, pretty much on deck all that ugly night.

The boat was so crowded with merchandise as to make walking up and down impossible. Even the master of it had to climb from one part of the vessel to another, and when two climbers met, one of them had to go back. My companions were rough, but they were not quarrelsome. They were about a dozen in all, and while some went to sleep in the rain, half-sheltered by bales of goods, others huddled together in the 'cabin', a dark and grimy bunk about as inviting as a coal cellar. I tried it for a few minutes; only a few. I slept by snatches, always to start up shivering. I have had wearier nights since then, but never one so long and miserable. Beyond the tramp of the horse (it seemed to grow louder as the animal disappeared into the darkness) and an occasional shout from the man who guided it, there was no sound to break the stillness. I could have fancied myself on land, with no companion but a soaking rain that fell softly and silently upon the deck, making puddles among the goods. Heavy drops or a rush of wind would have been a relief.

Day broke at last, and soon afterwards the rain stopped. I was too saturated, however, to take much notice of my surroundings now, and my fellow-travellers—most of them as wet as myself—left me alone. It would have done all of us a world of good had we got out and helped to tug the boat along, but no one even landed to stretch his limbs. We might have done so, for there were a number of locks to pass; but all energy had been washed out of us. Only the experienced travellers took off their coats to wring the water out of them. One I remember, paid the same attention to his shirt. Whether the sun shone that day I do not know. With occasional stoppages, we were dragged along between dripping fields, past villages; slowly it wore on to near night again. Except that there were less rain, the second night was as dreary as the first.

About eight o'clock in the morning we were on the outskirts of Glasgow, and there we disembarked. A more wretched-looking company, I should say, never slunk away from the water's edge. My teeth were chattering, and I do not know now how I managed to totter as far as the Broomielaw. Here I got into the ship that was to convey me to Liverpool, and the first part of the journey was nearly as slow as that on the canal. Once past Greenock, however, we went at good speed; and Liverpool was reached in thirty-six hours—almost exactly the same time as was taken to go between Edinburgh and Glasgow, a distance of some forty miles.

Slamannan Railway

Causewayend Basin.
East Dunbartonshire Libraries: The William Patrick Library, Kirkintilloch.

By the mid-1830s, rails stretched east from Glasgow to coal workings on the moors to the east of Airdrie. They were made up of the Garnkirk & Glasgow Railway, the Monkland & Kirkintilloch and its Kipps Branch line, and the Ballochney Railway. The Ballochney line was opened for traffic in 1827 and was subsequently used to send large quantities of coal to Edinburgh by way of the Monkland & Kirkintilloch and the canals, although at its eastern end it was as close to the Union Canal as the Forth & Clyde. The next logical development therefore was to continue the railway eastwards to Causewayend, near the Avon Aqueduct. As well as opening up a quicker and cheaper route to Edinburgh, the promoters of this new line hoped to exploit coal reserves on the bleak Slamannan plateau, but an initial survey of the reserves was unpromising. Despite this they pressed ahead, keeping their plan quiet until the last minute in the hope of receiving parliamentary approval before rivals could stop it with counter proposals. It worked and the Slamannan Railway Act was passed in 1835. The Ballochney Railway and Union Canal Companies had borne most of the cost.

Towards the end of 1838, with the railway under construction, the committee of management began to consider using the line for passengers. They had initially intended coal trains to be horse-hauled, but instead decided to order locomotives and made plans to take people from Glasgow to Causewayend by train, and from there to Edinburgh by boat. The service was inaugurated at the end of July 1840, with the train and boat getting their passengers to Edinburgh in four hours and back to Glasgow in time for dinner. A prosperous future seemed assured, but stagecoach operators stepped in to offer a better service between Edinburgh and Causewayend and the railway switched to favouring them. Train crews were instructed to leave Causewayend on time, whether the boat from Edinburgh had arrived or not. The Union Canal Company, faced with the prospect of their passengers being stranded in the middle of nowhere, had little alternative but to revert to canal-only services and cut fares to compete with the railway they had helped to create.

Despite reneging on their canal partners, the railway's passenger service did not prosper and was stopped just before the main Edinburgh & Glasgow Railway was opened in 1842. Early freight traffic was also disappointing, but the pessimistic early predictions for the coalfield were confounded when numerous collieries opened up around Slamannan and Standburn. Much of their rich splint coal went west to the ironworks of the Monklands, and some went long distances to other markets by rail to avoid the expense of having to transship to canal boats. Some traffic was attracted eastwards by reduced rates, but hardly ever enough to justify the splendid basin at Causewayend.

Edinburgh & Glasgow Railway

The parish ministers who compiled the *New Statistical Account* around 1840 all wrote of the Union Canal as being a burden to its promoters, whose enterprise had not been rewarded with the traffic to justify their outlay. The ministers were right; the canal had opened up new supplies of coal for Edinburgh and passengers had made good use of it, but it was not a commercial success. There was no industry of any size on it and, with railways expanding, the beleaguered company had no prospect of revival. It engaged in a costly campaign of opposition in an attempt to stall proposals for the Edinburgh & Glasgow Railway (E&G) going through Parliament, but failed and the line was authorised in 1838. There were some short-term gains from the sale of land to the railway and the use of boats by contractors to move heavy materials, but as the new line

EDINBURGH & GLASGOW RAILWAY

COALS

JAMES MACN .UGHTON begs leave to inform the a habitants of Edinburgh, that he has taken advantage of the facilities afforded by this Railway for bringing into Town, in a fresh state, the **COAL** of the Redding Coalfield.

The Coals derived from that field are of first quality; and as the Railway affords the means of procuring the Coal fresh from the Pits every day, both in Summer and Winter, J. M. is confident that his Establishment, at the Railway Depot, Hay Market, has only to be tried, to be found to supply an article superior to any yet brought into Edinburgh.

THE FOLLOWING ARE THE PRICES OF SEVERAL OF THE COALS AT THE DEPOT

Duke, of Hamilton's Hard or Splint Coal,	9s. 6d.
Do. Do. Soft Coal,	9s. 6d.
Craigend Splint Coal,	9s. 6d.
Do. Soft Coal,	9s. 6d.
Standrig Splint Coal,	9s. 6d.

Cartage, to all places within the Tolls, One Shilling additional.

A rise upon the Price of COALS at the Pits is anticipated very shortly; and Mr MACNAUGHTON recommends Families to supply themselves with COAL before such rise takes place.

Orders sent by Post to JAMES MACNAUGHTON, Edinburgh and Glasgow Railway Depot, or left at the Railway Company's Office, 6 South St Andrew Street; JOHN MACDOUGALL'S, 18 Howe Street; JOHN HILL'S, 60 Broughton Street; SCOUGALL & DRYSDALE'S, 223 High Street; ALEXANDER FERGUSON'S, 1 Melbourne Place; JOHN MACDOUGALL'S, 57 Niddry Street; D. REDPATH'S, 36 Nicolson Street; A. GILLON & SONS', 64 Grassmarket; and R. L. REID'S, 147 Princes Street,---will be punctually attended to.

NOTE.---The Time when the Coals are sent from the Depot is marked on the Railway Company's Ticket of Weight; and Mr MACNAUGHTON requests that any undue delay in delivering the Coals, or any incivility on the part of his Carters or Porters, may be intimated to him.

EDINBURGH AND GLASGOW RAILWAY DEPOT,
Hay Market, October 10, 1842.

James Brydone, Printer, 17 Hanover Street.

took shape beside the canal it must have presented an increasingly conspicuous threat.

The line opened in 1842 and passengers quickly switched to the faster, more comfortable trains. The Canal Company responded by reducing fares, but it was a hopeless gesture and passenger services were abandoned in 1848. Freight rates were also dropped, resulting in a temporary increase in the carriage of some commodities. Coal traffic kept going strongly for a time, with more than twice the amount being shipped into Edinburgh by canal in 1845 than by the E&G. Despite this their combined totals were being outstripped by new railways bringing coal from the great Midlothian coalfield into the city from the south and east. The canal's very reason for existence was under threat and the outlook was bleak.

The E&G also ran parallel with the Forth & Clyde and took trade from it too, but the prospect of unfettered competition damaging all three companies led them to negotiate a survival package. The Forth & Clyde was to take over the Union—debts and all—and the combined canal company would amalgamate with the railway, but the scheme collapsed in acrimony. Instead the Union Canal Company entered into an arrangement with the E&G which resulted in the railway taking over the canal in 1849. It was a curious thing to do; the canal was beaten and the price paid was well in excess of its value as a commercial waterway. The railway also had to honour an Act of Parliament which authorised the take-over, but required the canal to be kept in working condition.

The Forth & Clyde Fights Back

One canal company amalgamation did take place in 1846 when the Forth & Clyde took over the Monkland Canal. However, the E&G's take-over of the Union effectively set the inter-city canals in competition with each other. It was not in the Forth & Clyde's interest to send goods to Edinburgh on a rival system and so traffic went to the capital by way of the Forth estuary.

It was also evident that while steam was being used to the railway's advantage, it had never been successful on the canal, and so another experiment in towing passage boats was tried in 1845. The vessel used was a paddle tug called *Firefly*. She had two wheels on either side driven by an endless chain, and although the system appears to have worked the trials came to an end when the Forth & Clyde Canal Company discontinued passenger services in the late 1840s. The decision to stop passenger boats left communities not served by the railway without transport, and the challenge of providing a canal service for them was taken up by two individuals. One, a former skipper, appears to have failed, but the other, Alexander Taylor of the Eagle Inn, Kirkintilloch, succeeded in operating a boat between Port Dundas and Lock 20. Taylor had some experience of the boats: he had been a postilion on the swift horses, had hired horses to the company, and had been their ticket agent. In 1852, as A. & J. Taylor, a company formed with Falkirk ship-owner James Taylor, he extended the passenger service to Lock 16 with two boats.

While the Taylors were bucking the trend, the long struggle to find an alternative to horse-haulage came to a triumphant conclusion when a steam engine and screw propeller were fitted to the iron lighter, *Thomas*, in 1856. Screw propulsion proved to be a huge success and many other boats were speedily converted to it. The first new boat to be fitted with steam engine and propeller was the *Glasgow*. She was built at the Kelvin Dock boatyard at Maryhill in

Ratho

blether at the bridge

The hot gossip in Ratho in 1864 was the hanging of local carter George Bryce for the brutal murder of a young woman, Jane Seaton, who had maligned him to a girlfriend he was courting. His was the last public hanging in Edinburgh, an event which moved one contemporary scribe to verse:

> Take warning sweet maidens; let this be understood,
> Don't make a man angry—it'll do you no good,
> And gentlemen try to keep anger in check,
> Or you'll end like George Bryce with a rope round your neck.

The impact of rail: a canalside industry supplying a canalside town by rail!

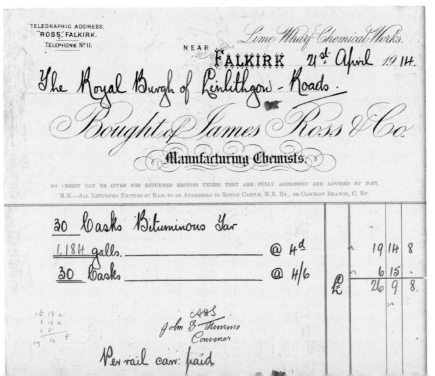

1857, significantly for use between Port Dundas and Leith, perhaps emphasising the Forth & Clyde's preference for that route to Edinburgh. In 1859 A. & J. Taylor replaced their horse-drawn passenger boats between Port Dundas and Lock 16 with a screw steamer, *Rockvilla Castle*. The canal and its various operators were not about to capitulate to the railways.

Railways Take Over

New railways were spreading rapidly across the country and the Forth & Clyde Canal Company faced competition on more than just the main inter-city route. They met it head on by opening their own railway in 1860. It went from Grangemouth Docks to near Grahamston on the Stirlingshire Midland Junction Railway which ran between Polmont and Larbert Junction. That line was operated by the E&G who, by a quirk of commercial convenience, also ran the Canal Company's railway for them.

The Canal Company made the Grangemouth Railway as a way of keeping control of the dock trade and they were right to see that as the key to their fortunes. The Carron had been deepened and straightened and the docks extended in the 1840s. Grangemouth had grown from nothing to become the principal port on the Forth and was in effect an eastern extension of Glasgow. And it was that city's great Caledonian Railway Company that took a keen interest in it.

The Caledonian and the Edinburgh-based North British Railway (NBR) had grown by the mid-1860s to become Scotland's big two railway companies. In their struggle for supremacy, they acquired many small companies including the E&G which, despite earlier attempts to amalgamate with the Caledonian, became, along with the Union Canal, part of the NBR system in 1865. The Caledonian's hopes of building up their presence in the east were dented by their rival's acquisition of the E&G, but not halted. They needed access to an east coast port and Grangemouth was ideal. The Forth & Clyde Canal Company, however, was not prepared to part with its prime asset on its own, and instead sold the entire Forth & Clyde and Monkland Canal system, including the branch railway from Grahamston. The NBR objected, but the Act of Parliament authorising the transfer of the undertaking and all of its assets was passed in 1867. The two canals were now owned by rival railways, but while the NBR had a failing waterway on its hands, the Forth & Clyde had never been busier.

The Caledonian had a dilemma; it had bought the canal, but not the privately operated boats whose owners only paid dues for the cargoes they carried. The railway could not therefore monopolise canal income as it could with trains and had good reason to shift goods onto rail, but it was not as simple as that. If it neglected the canal, the NBR's proximity meant that it was that railway which was most likely to profit, and so the Caledonian used the canal to compete. Inevitably trade declined, but it did not collapse and the canal settled into a trading pattern that sustained it into the twentieth century.

Grangemouth Docks.

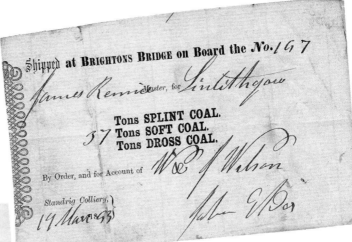

Shipped at BRIGHTONS BRIDGE on Board the No. *1 6 7*

James Rennie Master, for *Linlithgow*

Tons SPLINT COAL.
5 7 Tons SOFT COAL.
Tons DROSS COAL.

By Order, and for Account of *W & J Wilson*

Standrig Colliery,
19 March 93

Opposite: **Port Dundas Sugar Refinery, City of Glasgow Grain Mills and Stores and Canal Company offices at Spiers Wharf, Port Dundas, with coal scows waiting to unload at Port Dundas Generating Station.**

City of Glasgow Libraries and Archives; The Mitchell Library.

Pinkston Power Station.

Redding Colliery.

Scottish Mining Museum.

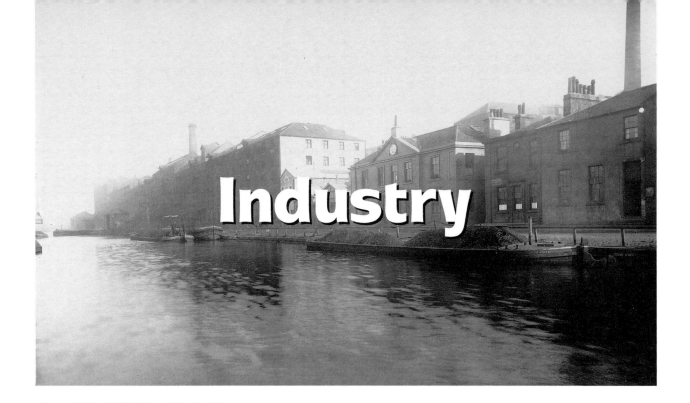

Industry

The canals were commercial highways, made to earn an income through trade; industry was vital to them. On the Forth & Clyde, factories, foundries, mines and mills, using or producing coal, chemicals, iron, timber or agricultural produce were set up from one side of the country to the other. They thrived thanks to the size of the canal and its links to the sea, while the extent and variety of industry helped the canal to prosper. The Union and Monkland Canals, both dependant on one or two major industries, did not fare so well.

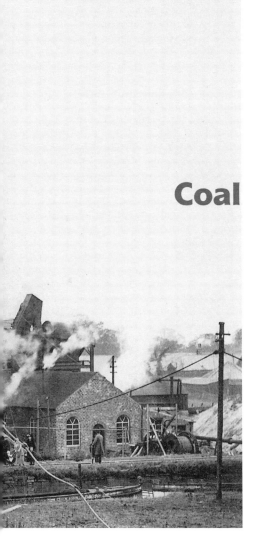

Coal

From the early days pits were opened up beside the River Carron and along the Forth & Clyde to beyond Glasgow. The coal went to wherever there was a market. Mines at Banknock supplied Glasgow, while Banton coal went to Carron and as far south as Whitby. Coal from Newcastle came into Bainsford and Clackmannan's coalmasters started to send coal to Glasgow as soon as the canal opened. The small pits to the west of Glasgow were given reduced carriage rates in the 1830s to help them compete with the large Govan Colliery for coal sales on the Clyde. With this and more added to the vast quantities of Monklands coal pouring west into Glasgow and beyond, it seems as if coal was constantly on the move in all directions.

The Union's principal coal workings were at its west end where pits at Redding, Middlerig and on the Polmont Braes employed around 400 men soon after the canal opened. These sent large amounts of coal to Edinburgh as well as to canalside towns and villages which had previously relied on supplies carted overland from Harthill. By the later nineteenth century the mines had worked out the coal close to the surface and the industry had to sink deeper shafts. Landowners leased their mineral rights to big companies who developed large collieries at Standburn, Maddiston and Redding. Smaller mines continued in the Falkirk area and one of these to the west of Bantaskine Bridge caused panic in 1877 when the old workings were thought to be close to collapse. The mine

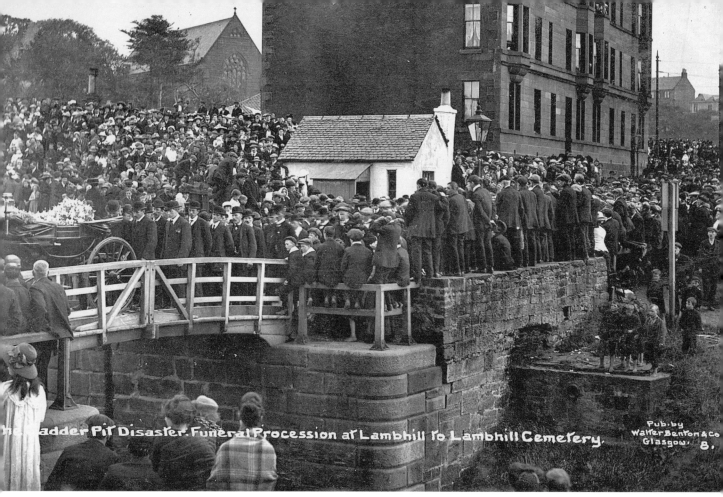

Mca. adder Pit Disaster. Funeral Procession at Lambhill to Lambhill Cemetery.

Pub. by
Walter Benton & Co
Glasgow. 8.

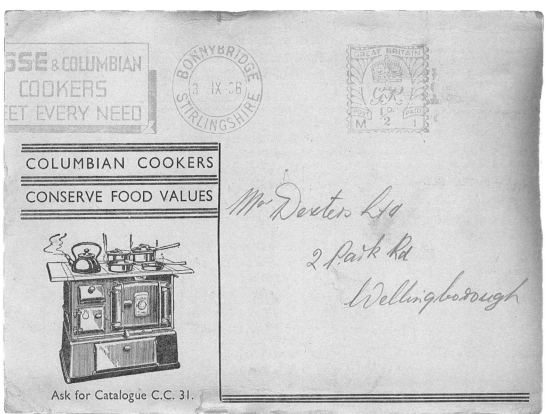

Trade card from Smith & Wellstood's Ironworks.

Smith & Wellstood's Foundry and Works at Bonnybridge.

Funeral procession for the victims of the Cadder mine disaster crossing Lambhill Bridge

ran under the canal and acted as a channel for a stream which supplied water to the town. A consultant mining engineer was called in, but to everyone's relief pronounced it deep enough to be of no immediate danger to the canal.[1]

The area around Kilsyth and Twechar developed into a prime location for high-grade coals and one of the country's deepest pits, St Flannan's, was sunk beside the canal to the west of Twechar. This and other industrial-scale pits produced huge quantities of coal, but as time wore on more and more of it left the collieries in railway wagons instead of boats.

Gasworks and power stations were amongst the last users of canal-borne coal. Pinkston Power Station's cooling tower was the second largest in Europe and discharged warm water back into what local children called the 'hot canal'. It was a pleasing if dirty and not wholly safe place to swim, but there was also money to be made. Boys paddled on home-made rafts to where high-grade coal had spilled from the power station loading point. They dived into the warm water to retrieve it and then, using an old pram or bogie, hawked the fuel round people's houses for pocket money!

Two of Scotland's worst pit disasters happened beside the canals. In 1923, 40 men died when water from old flooded underground workings burst into Redding No. 23 pit, and 22 died in 1913 when fire broke out at the Carron Company's Cadder No. 15 pit, near Bishopbriggs.

The men who worked at the Cadder and other adjacent pits lived in villages or single rows scattered along the canal between Bishopbriggs and Lambhill. Their names have now all but disappeared: Mavis Valley, Jellyhill, Lochfauld Rows (also known as the Shangie, or Shanghai Rows) and Kenmure, a single row of twelve two-room cottages across the canal from Lochfauld. The men from Kenmure Row used a primitive 'punt' to cross the canal. They hauled it over by means of a fixed chain which when not in use sank to the bottom to keep the channel clear. A story is also told of there being a spirit shop at Lochfauld run by the mining company, but, because drinking on the premises was not allowed, the men used the punt to cross to 'The Big Room', a field where they sat and drank. In later years they walked to pubs at Lambhill, Bishopbriggs or Torrance, and when they returned home sometimes swam across the canal when drink persuaded them that using the punt was too much trouble. It was removed in 1929 after the pits had closed.[2]

Ironworking

Canalside pits like Possil and Hamilton Hill worked ironstone, and some, like the Carron Company's Nethercroy pit, extracted both iron and coal.

The Carron Company's early relationships with the Forth & Clyde Canal Company were not always harmonious, but neither company let that get in the way of business. From the early days there was a Carron Company wharf and warehousing at Port Dundas, and basins in Falkirk with, over the years, road, tramway and railway connections to the Carron works. The company's boats could also take a short-cut from the river to the Forth & Clyde at Lock 3 along a small canal known as the Carron Cut.

Carron and other early ironworks were equipped with coal-hungry, cold-blast furnaces which produced expensive iron, but when James Beaumont Neilson developed the hot-blast process of smelting in 1828 it transformed Scotland's iron industry. A wave of unfettered expansion swept the Monklands. The area was rich in blackband ironstone and when this was used with raw splint coal in hot-blast furnaces it produced abundant

A Carron Company lighter approaching Lock 5 past Castlelaurie Ironworks, Bainsford.

Industrial Broxburn seen from Miss Margaret's Bridge.
West Lothian Libraries

Dougal's Brickworks at Winchburgh.

cheap iron. Coatbridge became the country's iron capital: Gartsherrie Ironworks was set up in 1831 and others followed at Summerlee, Calder, Dundyvan, and Langloan. They were all beside the Monkland Canal, as were numerous malleable ironworks. With all of them using canal water for cooling, and returning it while it was still warm, the canal literally steamed. Coatbridge, filled with fire, steam, noise and smoke was aptly described as 'hell with the lid off'.

Carron quickly converted its furnaces to hot blast, but had to compete with many new rivals. Foundries were set up beside the Forth & Clyde Canal because it gave access to Grangemouth Docks and was ideal for moving heavy raw materials in and finished castings out. Indeed, there were so many works in Falkirk, Bonnybridge, Kirkintilloch and Glasgow that between them they accounted for 50 per cent of the British light iron castings industry.

Iron was not a major industry on the Union, but there was a small works at Causewayend Basin. It no doubt drew fuel and raw material along the Slamannan Railway from the same sources that supplied the huge Monklands industry.

Shale Oil

The shale oil industry made scant use of the Union Canal, despite many large works being in close proximity to it. The industry began in 1850 when James 'Paraffin' Young first extracted oil from Bathgate cannel coal. When that began to run out he sought an alternative and, after 'discovering' shale, set up the Addiewell oilworks. After his patent expired in 1864 the industry expanded rapidly, with major works being set up beside the canal at Broxburn, Winchburgh and further west at Philpstoun. The scale of their operations can be gauged from the size of the bings of spent shale that form part of the canal landscape in West Lothian.[3]

Although the industry made little use of the canal, it did pollute it from time to time. In 1893 and again in 1949 complaints about dead farm animals or fish were traced to the large oilworks at Pumpherston, some distance from the canal. In the later incident, poor effluent control from the manufacture of detergent contaminated the River Almond and the effects spread down the feeder lade and along to Broxburn and Winchburgh.

Bricks

There were a number of brickworks adjacent to both canals, but Dougal's Brickworks at Winchburgh is perhaps the one that used the canals most. It was set up in the mid-nineteenth century to make bricks from the area's abundant blue clay, and the output was taken by boat to Edinburgh and other markets. The company had its own stables and its horses could be changed at other locations when they got tired, although the men had to sleep on board their boats and keep going until the job was done.[4]

Stone

Quarries were opened to supply stone for the construction of the Forth & Clyde Canal and some continued in operation providing cargoes and revenue after its opening. Kilsyth became a centre for the industry with a whinstone quarry at Strone Point which was worked for rubble stone, and another at Auchinstarry that provided many of Glasgow's kerbstones and remained in operation up to the 1960s. Freestone was quarried at Balgray on the west side of Glasgow, and a quay was built for the quarry in 1825 beside the Kelvin Aqueduct. Possil Quarry was shipping so much stone at a wharf in the narrow channel to the east of Lambhill Bridge that the Canal Company asked for the

Cart boat on the Forth & Clyde Canal.

Mill at Rockvilla: drawing by William Power.
City of Glasgow Libraries and Archives; The Mitchell Library.

Grangemouth timber basins.

trade to be shifted to the west side and for care to be taken not to let stone fall in the canal!

Lime was also worked adjacent to the canal and there was a large limeworks at Netherwood on a cut running off the canal just to the west of Wyndford stop-lock. A drawbridge across the entrance was removed in 1788 on condition that it would be replaced if the south bank of the canal was needed for tracking ice boats.

Landowners close to the Union Canal got quite a bonus when stone for the big structures was quarried on their ground, but the industry really came into its own when the canal was opened. Edinburgh was growing and needed supplies of building stone, paving and lime. Large whinstone and greywacke quarries were opened on either side of the canal at Ratho, but some of the waste was thrown into the canal and boats were damaged before the water could be run off and the obstruction cleared. Much of Edinburgh was said to have been cobbled with Ratho stone and the quarries also supplied building stone, road metal, gravel and builders' sand. They were only accessible by canal, but loaded barges often went only about a mile to the west, to Wilkie's Basin, where their cargoes were unloaded onto carts and taken to the railway at Bathgate.

An article in the *West Lothian Courier* in 1878 described the loading of stone near Woodcockdale, much of which probably came from Kettlestoun.

> There was a jetty on the north bank for causewaying [whinstone cobbles] and macadamising stones [whin chips], and one further west, on the south bank, for loading limestone and limeshell from Bowden Hill. To the east of Linlithgow was Kingscavil Quarry and just outside Edinburgh were the great freestone quarries of Redhall and Hailes, the latter being worked to a depth of over 100 feet.[5]

One sad story from the Union's stone trade concerns George Meikle Kemp, the architect of the Scott Monument. He was working on its construction when he visited a contractor one foggy evening in March 1844 and then set off back to his lodgings in the city. He never made it and his drowned body was found in the canal at Fountainbridge the following day.

Timber was needed for the construction industry and boat-building, and started coming in to the Forth & Clyde Canal as soon as it was open. The principal source was the Baltic, but North American timber also came into the canal from the Clyde and some was brought 'north about' through the Pentland Firth to Grangemouth. There the timber was stored in huge ponds situated in the angle between the expanding docks and the main channel. Sawn planks were taken through the canal on lighters, but large logs were simply strapped together and towed as rafts. These could be 60 feet long, sixteen feet wide and draw four feet of water, and when that mass was on the move it was not easy to stop! Timber merchants left the wood in the water to maintain its moisture content while it seasoned, but by 1788 so much was coming into Glasgow that it was clogging up the Hamilton Hill Basin. To solve the problem, a special timber basin was made on the outside of the long bend at Firhill and another was excavated in 1844 on the inside of the bend. Some of the large canalside timber yards at Grangemouth, Port Dundas and Temple continued to operate up to and beyond the canal's closure.

Great Canal Brewery, Glasgow.

Miss Townie, Appin House.

To Hugh Baird & Co.

1819.

Sec. 23   To Amt, of A/o rendered,   11 1 7

Sec. 30   By £/C,   11 1 7

Hugh Baird & Co
Jno. Aitken

A link between the two canals—a bill sent from a Forth & Clyde Canal based industry to the Union Canal chairman's Appin House.

Transport contrasts and distillery at Port Dundas.

City of Glasgow Libraries and Archives; The Mitchell Library.

Agriculture

Getting basic foodstuffs to where people lived was a huge step forward made possible by the canals, and grain from Europe, England and the east coast of Scotland was being shipped along the Forth & Clyde Canal as soon as it opened. Bainsford became a large grain storage and distribution point, while flour mills, bakeries and factories making feedstuffs and other agricultural products were established at Port Dundas.

Some farmers had their own jetty and could move produce in their own boats. The Canal Company also devised a boat to carry loaded farm carts and animals so that farmers could move goods directly to markets.

The Union Canal opened up Edinburgh to producers and one trader was quick to capitalise on this by renting a warehouse at Port Hopetoun for the import and sale of agricultural produce. Mills on the Rivers Avon and Almond were able to send their products to Edinburgh more easily, while tanneries in Linlithgow and Falkirk brought in their raw materials from the city and sent the finished goods back. Farms also benefited from boats leaving the cities loaded with manure. Dung boats, as they were called, went from Redhall manure wharf to farms as far west as Polmont.

Brewing and Distilling

Distilleries needed plenty of cooling water and reliable supplies of grain and coal, which made canalsides ideal locations for them. There were distilleries at Port Dundas, Falkirk (Rosebank), Underwood, Banknock (Bankier), Bowling, and on the Union Canal at Linlithgow and Edinburgh. They seem to have been vulnerable places. In June 1791 the Underwood maltings and a large quantity of malt and barley were destroyed by fire. Numerous volunteers and a fire engine from Falkirk used water from the canal to douse the flames, but everything was so dry it was quickly lost. A distillery at Port Dundas was blown down in a gale in 1818 and, when the Union Canal overflowed at The Mains in 1825, Mr Glen's distillery was swamped, resulting in damaged buildings and lost whisky![6]

In 1810 so many Port Dundas distilleries were discharging waste water into the basin that local inhabitants and ships' masters complained that the water was unfit for human consumption, and petitioned the Canal Company to provide a separate fresh water supply. At the time municipal water supplies were at best rudimentary and the canal was regarded as a suitable source of drinking water. While it would not have been stirred up by boats' propellers or subject to oil spills, it would nevertheless have been polluted by discarded rubbish and other waste.

The ubiquitous Baird family founded the Great Canal Maltings and Great Canal Brewery on sites adjacent to the Old Basin in the 1820s and subsequently developed other maltings, stores and a roasting house in the Port Dundas area. The canal at the original maltings was described in the late 1880s as having 'a string of barges filled with sacks of barley' on it.[7]

Canal towns and villages were noted for the consumption of strong drink. The quarrying village of Ratho had fourteen pubs—the Pop Inn was reputed to be so-named because boatmen could simply pop in through one door, down a dram and hasten out of another door while the horse kept going. Kirkintilloch's wayward ways caught up with it in 1921 when the inhabitants voted to banish drink from the town, and it remained dry until 1968.

The Great Canal Brewery by T.C.F. Brotchie.

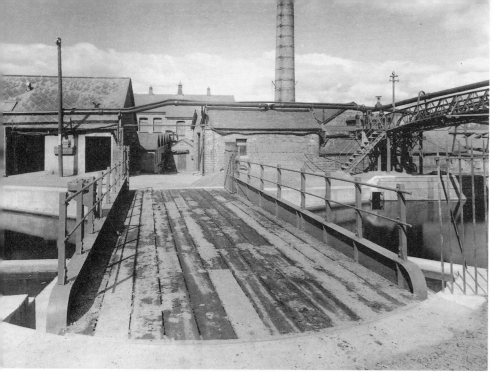

Nobel's chemical works at Redding.
Crown Copyright: Royal Commission on the Ancient and Historical Monuments of Scotland (Sir William Arrol Collection).

Making boots at the North British Rubber Co.'s Castle Mills.

Dalmuir, with Somervail & Co.'s Bridge and Roof Works on the left and the Singer sewing machine factory at Clydebank in the distance. Singer's was the largest manufacturing concern on either canal. It was established in 1885 and at its peak occupied a 110 acre site with 3,000,000 square feet of floor space and a workforce of 14,000 people. It closed in 1980.

Chemicals

Glasgow's tallest chimney at Townsend's Port Dundas chemical works.

Port Downie became a centre for chemical industries and lists of vessels passing Lock 16 before the First World War indicate a healthy trade in kelp and 'muriates of potash'. The former was burned to produce the latter which is better known today as potassium chloride. At Lime Wharf, about a mile west of Lock 16, James Ross set up a works which imported crude tar, refined it and also made naphtha and pitch. Ross had early associations with the boatyard at Port Downie and had a special tar-carrying vessel designed there, but the yard closed before she could be made. Instead she was built at Kirkintilloch and launched as the *Aniline* in 1889.[8] She was in regular use up to 1920 as probably the only purpose-built chemical carrier on the canal, although three tanker lighters, the *Mexdee*, *Clydegate* and *Perfection* carried oil through the canal from terminals on the Clyde. The Lime Wharf works expanded its range of products through the late nineteenth and early twentieth centuries and was still being operated by the Scottish Tar Distillers until a disastrous fire in 1973 hastened its closure.[9]

Nobel's Explosives Company Ltd., formed in 1876, had a large works beside the Union Canal at Redding, and set up another works at Linlithgow (although not beside the canal) in the early 1900s. The company was absorbed into Imperial Chemical Industries (ICI) which concentrated its explosives operations at Ardeer in Ayrshire in the 1930s.

There were chemical industries in Kirkintilloch, and Glasgow's northern skyline was dominated by Charles Tennant and Joseph Townsend's chemical factories at St Rollox and Port Dundas. These works had the city's two tallest chimneys and their position to the north of the main urban centre meant that the prevailing south-westerly wind carried the smoke and fumes away from it, although the developing Springburn area was not so lucky!

Later industries, unable to find space at Port Dundas, were set up adjacent to Ruchill Bridge where they could also spew out atmospheric pollutants and not affect the city. Alexander Ferguson's Glasgow Lead & Colour Works was on either side of the bridge and Bryant & May's match factory was just to the west. John Sandeman's Ruchill Oil Works clung to a sloping site between Murano Street and Bilsland Drive and the Glasgow Rubber Works of George MacLellan & Co. was just to the east of Ruchill Bridge. The Ioco Proofing Company also operated a rubber works close to the canal at Netherton to the west of Glasgow.

In Edinburgh an American entrepreneur took over the vacant Castle Silk Mill at Fountainbridge in 1855 and established the North British Rubber Co. It was the biggest manufacturing concern on the Union Canal, taking in raw rubber and making a variety of products from it. The works also spawned the nearby Scottish Vulcanite Company in 1861.

Glass and Pottery

The chemicals and drinks industries needed a variety of containers, some of which were made locally in potteries and cooperages adjacent to the canal.

There was an extensive glass industry beside the Forth & Clyde's Glasgow Branch. The Caledonian and Firhill Glass Bottle Works sat on either side of Chance Brother's Glasgow Glass Works at Ruchill and there were other works and warehouses round the corner at Firhill and Hamilton Hill. Sand was brought in by lighter and loaded directly into the works—a 'hell-hole' where furnaces never cooled and shifts of workers kept production going round the clock and the calendar. The former glass-making site at Ruchill is now occupied by Glasgow University's Murano Street Student Village—the street was named after the famous glass-making Murano Island near Venice!

Maryhill from across the Kelvin Aqueduct.

Kelvin Dock doubled as a timber yard and during the Disruption of 1843 when the Free Church of Scotland split from the Established Church, the saw pit was used for Free Church services. It was jokingly referred to as Maryhill Cathedral.

Sometime around 1810, the dock lessee turned his house at the upper basin into a pub which became a popular haunt for boatmen, whose rowdy behaviour made it an unpopular one for the locals. In common with other canalside towns, Maryhill was noted for the consumption of strong drink with one public house to every 59 inhabitants! Mary Hill's grandson, John Dunlop, an unpopular absentee landlord, was so appalled by what he saw on occasional visits to the area that he founded one of Britain's first temperance societies there in 1829. It had little impact on the hard-living locals, but by contrast the large number of navvies who came to build railways and lay Glasgow's water pipes in the 1850s made a huge impression. Drunken lawlessness took over and civic leaders appealed to Glasgow for help, but the city declined and so they applied for police burgh status. It was granted in 1856.[10]

The following year the newly installed constabulary had to deal with the theft of coal and potatoes from boats moored in the centre of the boatyard basin for security. The robbers used a small boat to get on board, and as ever, miners, so often the butt of nineteenth century outrage, got the blame.[11]

Canal Town

Most canalside communities were associated with one industry or another, but few could really be described as canal towns. On the Union Canal, Ratho and Redding came closest, although their main concern was with extractive industries, while Broxburn and Winchburgh were mainly oil towns with a canal flowing past them. The canal was hardly noticed by Linlithgow and it made relatively little impact on Edinburgh.

The Forth & Clyde created Grangemouth although the docks outgrew the canal, while at the west end Bowling developed links to the Clyde. Parts of Falkirk were shaped by the canal, while Bonnybridge and Twechar had associations with it but were concerned with other industries. Kirkintilloch predated the canal, but shaped much of its history and can fairly claim to be a canal town. Port Dundas eventually outgrew the canal, which leaves Maryhill as the only town or village that was created by either canal and developed and declined in complete harmony with it. The burgh coat of arms even features a canal event that never happened, the *Charlotte Dundas* crossing the Kelvin Aqueduct.

Maryhill grew up around the flight of locks that dropped down from the summit to the Kelvin Aqueduct. There was a Canal Company graving dock between the locks, known as Port Kelvin, Kelvin Dock, or simply the Dock. Later, when more land was needed for expansion, Robert Graham, whose wife Mary had inherited the Gairbraid Estate from her father Hew Hill, agreed to feu the ground on condition that the village should be 'in all times called the town of Mary Hill'.

The dock was at the heart of Maryhill and, according to the *Glasgow Courier*, was the centre of a dramatic rescue in September 1809. A boy who fell from a large brig as it passed through the locks disappeared below the surface. The clamour of people watching alerted Alexander Reid, an apprentice blacksmith at the dock, who ran to the water, jumped in fully clothed and saved the almost lifeless youth.[12]

The dock's clever positioning, between Locks 22 and 23, meant that it could be emptied into one of the lower basins through a culvert. Originally the culvert was opened and closed by a simple plug, but this was replaced by a sluice in 1826. There was a stables and a house for the ship's carpenter beside the dock—the first occupant was a John Drysdale from Carronshore. Hugh and Robert Baird, who took over the lease in 1800, sub-let it to Tam Morrison of Falkirk in 1807. When he died in 1816 his son John took over and in 1827 Archibald Blair leased the yard. It was taken over ten years later by David Swan who, with his sons, built up a thriving shipbuilding business which remained in the family until 1893. William and Charles MacNicoll took over at the dock in 1923. They built some yachts, repaired other craft and built landing craft during the Second World War. The yard closed in 1949.[13]

Maryhill's early mines were poor, wet affairs and so Monklands coal was brought by canal to a ree (coalyard) at the head of the locks and taken by cart to Milngavie and other communities to the north-west. Large quantities of coal from Twechar Colliery were brought to Dawsholm Gasworks by canal. As well as the gasworks, there was a large chemical works adjacent to the lock flight and a spelter works operated for a time beside the top lock (spelter is a copper-zinc alloy used in plumbing work and for ornamental castings). Ironworks to the east and west of Stockingfield Junction completed an industrial mix that mirrored that of the rest of the canal.

TO LET,
KELVIN DRY DOCK, HOUSE, SHEDS, &c.

Upon a Lease of Seven Years, from Whitsunday, 1820. THE advantages of the DOCK (being on the side of the Forth and Clyde Canal Navigation) are so well known that any explanation is unnecessary.

The Dock and Premises thereto belonging, will be shewn by Mr. Thomas Morrison, at the Dock; or John Robb, the Canal Company's Lock-keeper.

Sealed Offers, addressed to the Committee of Council for the Forth and Clyde Navigation, will be received until Thursday the 12th August; and, for any further particulars, application may be made at the Canal Office, Port-Dundas.

CANAL OFFICE, PORT-DUNDAS, 23d July, 1819.

The Kelvin Dock name lives on.

Early steam lighters c.1870: drawing by David Small.

Lighters at Port Dundas c.1870: drawing by David Small.

Working Boats

Repairing a lighter at J. & J. Hay's slip beside Kirkintilloch Basin.

Goods-carrying boats were unsophisticated barges known as lighters or scows. The Union Canal Company specified the 'common scow' in the 1820s as a vessel to carry a 40-ton load, 66 feet long, eleven feet broad and five feet deep. The keel was to be of Memel fir or American elm, and other timbers were to be elm, oak, beech or fir, all caulked with black oakum and finished with well warmed best Archangel tar, applied at least four days before launching. A loading index, proved by the company's weights, was to be fixed to the vessel. The owner's name and boat number were to be painted in white on a black ground at bow and stern, in four-inch high letters.

Scow is a Scots word for a flat-bottomed boat and is similar in sound and meaning to a Dutch word. The same word is also used in America to describe a lighter! So what's in a name? Smaller boats may have been called scows and larger ones lighters, there may have been geographical preferences for one or the other, but any substantial reason for the use of either word has been lost in time. After the advent of screw propulsion 'scow' seems to have been commonly applied to horse-drawn boats and 'lighter' to steam-powered craft. To add to the confusion, steam lighters were also known as 'screws' or 'puffers'. 'Puffer' comes from the puffing sound made by the early steam engines exhausting through the funnel and, despite the development of more sophisticated systems which meant they no longer puffed, the name stuck. These much-loved little vessels were immortalised by Neil Munro in his tales of *Para Handy and the Vital Spark*, and the film *The Maggie*. Different types of puffer, or lighter, were made for coastal trading and to go to island destinations or to Ireland; others stayed in sheltered esturial waters, while the simplest boats were confined to the Forth & Clyde Canal. They were all developed at little canalside boatyards.

Boat-building

Some boatyards were established early in canal history, others came later; some worked for a long time, others only briefly. The Forth & Clyde Canal Company

Launching a lighter at Hay's yard.

Logan on the stocks at Kelvin Dock.

One of the Bergius Company's motor launches undergoing trials at Bowling. The company, based at Port Dundas, was one of the longest lasting boat-building operations on either canal. They bought in the hulls of launches, fitted them out to customers' specifications and installed Kelvin Marine diesel engines. If the boats required dry docking they were sailed to Kelvin Dock, although a chain hoist was latterly used to lift the after ends of the boats out of the water at Port Dundas.

George Bergius.

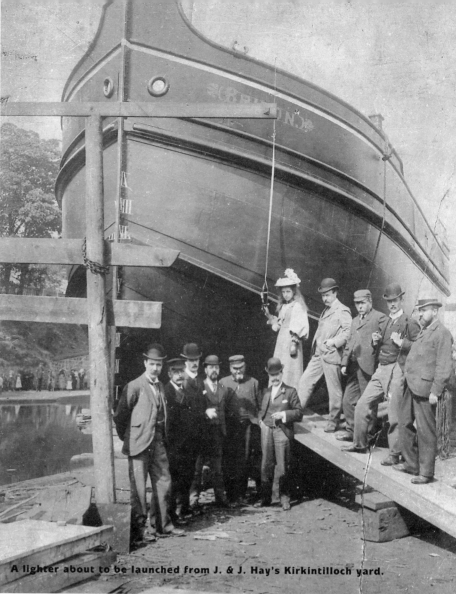

A lighter about to be launched from J. & J. Hay's Kirkintilloch yard.

A Bergius Company motor launch at their Port Dundas yard.

George Bergius.

Scow on the Union Canal at Polmont.
Bob McCutcheon.

A Union Canal scow negotiating the
Almond Aqueduct.

Firhill Bridge   Peter Stewart.

blether at the bridge

Firhill Bridge has had at least four names: Roughhill Easter, Napiershall, Firhill and the Nolly Brig, although it would have been crashed into just as often whatever its name. In 1833 the luggage boat *Appin* tried to go through with only one leaf raised and carried away the other, and in another incident the passage boats *Rapid* and *Vulcan* met at the bridge, got into a muddle, and damaged the towpath leaf. In January 1910 a steam lighter caught the bridge and ripped it down. In later years it was known as Jock's Brig after Jock Young, or 'Jock the Briggie' as he was better known.[3]

operated a depot, dock and boatyard at Tophill in Falkirk. The track-boats *Charlotte* and *Margaret* were built there and work was also done on *Charlotte Dundas*. Thomas Wilson, the builder of the pioneering iron boat *Vulcan*, became resident engineer at Tophill in 1822 and built more iron vessels there, including the track-boat *Cyclops*. The company made lock-gates at both Tophill and Port Dundas, but in 1831 decided to transfer the bulk of its Glasgow workforce to Tophill and concentrate lock-gate work there. Boat-building at the yard appears to have dwindled after the 1840s.

Thomas Wilson was succeeded at Tophill by his son Robert, and they both had an interest in the boatyard at Port Downie. It made numerous vessels, including a number of steam lighters, but closed in 1889 to make way for a railway extension. The principal boat-building operation on the Union Canal was the company's own yard at Gilmore Place, although there was a small boatyard and dry dock at the west side of the Avon Aqueduct. The dock was emptied by drawing a simple plug to let the water flow into the river.

Another early dock, at Bowling Basin, was initially leased by Thomas and William McGill, but closed in 1849 to allow the basin to be extended for the new sea lock. The *Savage*, launched by the McGills in 1800, is thought to be the first schooner built on the Clyde.

Boats appear to have been built at more than one location at Hamilton Hill. The main site was probably the slipway at the east end of the basin and this may be where the *Thomas*, the first lighter to be converted to steam screw propulsion, was fitted up in 1856. The uncertainty arises from the presence of another building slip on a side cut to the west. It is not clear when it was first established, but it was used between 1876 and 1903 by William Burrell & Co. (of Burrell Collection fame) to build lighters.

The boat regarded as the first puffer was the 39-ton screw propelled steam vessel built at Kelvin Dock in 1857, the *Glasgow*. She had a 65-foot long iron hull with a beam of seventeen feet and a hold depth of eight feet six inches. She was the start of a tradition at the yard that lasted into the early 1920s when its last puffers, *Logan* and *Kype*, were launched.[1]

The last puffer built on the canal was the *Chindit*, launched at the Kirkintilloch yard of J. Hay & Sons Ltd. in 1945. Boat-building had begun to the west of Townhead Bridge in 1865 and the yard was taken over by John Hay three years later. He, and succeeding generations of Hays, went on to build and operate one of the largest fleets of lighters on the canal. They also established an engineering shop at Port Dundas and had a repair slipway at Kirkintilloch which continued in operation up to 1962. A wide range of vessels was also built by Peter McGregor & Co. at their boatyard at Kirkintilloch Basin.

The Port Dundas basins were used for boat-building during the nineteenth century and, in the early 1900s, William Jack & Co. built lighters there. Two small yards beside the Grangemouth timber basins also built lighters and scows: William Drake's from 1885 to 1913 and David McGill's from 1902 to 1922.[2]

A scow at Winchburgh. Union Canal boatmen had to contend with silt, weeds and floating debris and were lucky to achieve 2 m.p.h. with a loaded boat and 3 m.p.h. unloaded.

Working the Boats

The Carron Company had a large fleet of boats and when one was dangerously overloaded with ironstone in 1826 it prompted a polite but pointed letter. Overloading was common and the Forth & Clyde Canal Company clearly wanted to stop the practice. Another exchange of letters in 1832 followed the Canal Company's suspicions that goods carried by Charles Tennant & Co. did not match what they were paying for. These were not big incidents, but they

At times it was difficult to control water levels in the Bainsford reach because of the number of vessels coming up through Lock 5 to the foundry and other businesses. In September 1868, on a day when the level had dropped by a few inches, the lighter *Express*, drawing eight feet four inches, went aground above Bainsford Bridge. While she was stuck the lighter *Onyx*, two Leith lighters, some rafts and other vessels were let up through Lock 5, further depleting the water. The skipper of the *Express* was not amused—his boat was failing to live up to its name—but even after the supervisor had let more water into the pound to refloat her he refused to go on until the full level had been reinstated. Anxious to get traffic moving again the supervisor tried to bring *Onyx* past the *Express*, but the angry skipper would not relinquish his place at the front of the line and pushed a man into the canal who had boarded his vessel to pass a rope to the *Onyx*. Two and a half hours after she had grounded, the *Express* was moving again.[3] It was a small incident, but it shows how important it was for men whose income depended on delivery to avoid hold-ups (and incidentally how busy the canal was at the time it was taken over by the Caledonian Railway).

Ice breaker and dredger *Clydeforth* in Lock 35.
East Dunbartonshire Libraries: The William Patrick Library, Kirkintilloch.

point to a culture of people pushing themselves and their boats hard, perhaps too hard, in an effort to make a living.

In the early days, boats on the Forth & Clyde worked long hours to make deliveries before winter set in, and newspapers carried advertisements advising potential users that the canal would remain open unless stopped by ice. When ice did form, considerable efforts were made to clear it, as in December 1791 when teams of eighteen or more horses were used to keep the company's 'ice-boats' working for two weeks. The cost was high and one boat was wrecked, but the navigation stayed open. There were other bad winters: in 1874/75 an ice-breaker, hauled by nineteen horses, took two days to get from Maryhill to Bowling. The boat stuck in heavy ice at Dalmuir on the way back and the attempt was abandoned. Ice-breakers were based at Glasgow and Grangemouth and in 1895, as they tried to work towards each other, the one coming west took a day to smash less than two miles of ice between Auchinstarry and Twechar. It was towed by 36 horses and its unpredictable movement threw some of the animals into the canal and one into a hedge where it was badly injured.[4]

It was often not worth the effort of breaking the ice because wooden-hulled boats could still be badly damaged, particularly if it had been broken into floes. Skippers often preferred to wait for ice to melt, which must have been doubly frustrating for them because freezing temperatures improved muddy roads and while they sat, carters were able to move more freely.[5] In later years a steam dredger and ice-breaker, the *Clydeforth*, was used to smash through the ice, often followed by a convoy of fishing boats. The fishermen strapped iron sheets round the waterline of their wooden vessels for added protection.

The Union Canal was prone to icing up because it was narrower, shallower and less well used and as a result there were many years when it was closed for long periods. It was kept clear, when possible, by a small ice boat which was weighted with slag and hauled by up to sixteen horses. One Union Canal passage boat bound for Edinburgh was stopped by snow at Broxburn in March 1827 when deep drifts blocked the tracking path making it impossible for the horse to continue. Passengers had to be put up in the town overnight.[6]

Ice apart, boat crews kept going regardless of the weather, but sometimes fell victim to bad conditions because they left holds uncovered. Gales in early March 1850 sank a number of scows in the canal and the River Carron.

The *Agnes* was overwhelmed while being towed into Carron Mouth and the crew were only saved with some difficulty. The *Ann* struggled along the 'four-mile-reach' from Underwood with whin metal for the Carron Company, but shipped water entering Lock 16 and went down. The *Falkirk* lay-to at Tophill for the night with a heavy deck-load of railway sleepers, but she was caught by high winds and went down in nine feet of water. Some trackers made a raft of the sleepers and rescued the crew. Gales drove the *Annie* onto a rock near Kirkintilloch in 1897 prompting tongue-in-cheek calls in the local newspaper for a lighthouse or lifeboat on the canal. High winds and heavy rain also sank a sand-laden scow at Hillhead in 1900 and the scow *Sally*, with a cargo of pig-iron, in Castlecary Lock in 1901. Another scow with a load of pig iron sank in 1928 in Hamilton Hill basin after sitting for some days in heavy rain. She just filled up and went down.[7]

Collisions between boats, and between boats and structures, were also part of canal life. Manoeuvring heavy unpowered vessels in confined waters was not easy and they often damaged fixtures and fittings. If deemed guilty,

A scow at South Bantaskine on the Union Canal surrounded by the kind of broken ice that made winter such a treacherous time for wooden-hulled boats.
Bob McCutcheon.

. . . sometimes boats just sank

A vessel loaded with iron went down about a mile west of Hamilton Hill Basin in 1791 and the *Alloa Packet* sank at Hungryside in 1819 and had to be broken up to be taken out. A lighter loaded with iron went down in Underwood Lock in 1874 stopping canal trade for a day and holding up the sailings of the steamers from Grangemouth to London and Rotterdam. The *Hannibal*, carrying pig-iron from Grangemouth to Glasgow in 1893, was holed near Kirkintilloch and sank at the Glasgow Road Bridge while the *Caesar*, with pig-iron for Ruchill, sprang a leak and sank near Stockingfield in 1897. The pig-iron laden scow *Betsy* sank in 1904 at Cadder and the steamer *Terrier* went down at Meiklehill with pig-iron and salt. The salt dissolved and she was raised in only twelve hours. In 1901 a passing steamer forced a scow loaded with timber into the sloping side at Twechar and, as it tipped, it shipped water and sank. The sloping banks did for J. & J. Hay's scow *Rose* in 1913 while she was being towed by a steam lighter. She swung too close to the side, tilted and filled up with water, much to the discomfort of the boatman whose breakfast was being prepared at the time.

The *Annie*'s cargo disappeared when she came to grief outside the Lochfauld miners' rows in 1914. Whisky, beer and an assortment of general goods was looted in a canal version of *Whisky Galore*. The forces of law arrived the following morning to secure the vessel, but had to content themselves with securing convictions for theft. The authorities reacted more speedily when the *Nellie* went down in 1918 at Auchendavy with a cargo of whisky and beer, and another steamer loaded with beer went down at Auchinstarry two years later.[8]

In many of these incidents the worst that happened to people was that they got wet, but when the *Hero*'s boiler blew up in 1897 the skipper and engineer were killed and a lock keeper was badly injured. The boat was heading west with a cargo of pig-iron for Lochburn Iron Foundry in Maryhill and was in Lock 4 when the explosion occurred. It blew the mate, who had gone ashore to work the lock sluices, into the water 30 yards away but he was able to swim to safety. The blast broke windows in nearby houses and two women were injured by flying debris. A sleeping man escaped with only a rude awakening when a piece of iron landed beside his bed. Iron smashed through the roof of the adjacent Abbots Iron Foundry narrowly missing some moulders and warehousemen. *Hero* sank. She was a new boat fitted with a second-hand boiler, and the inquiry found that the accident had happened because the safety valve had been tampered with to improve speed. It was common practice, but the consequences were not normally so dreadful.[9]

A crewman from the oil boat *Clydegate* swinging on the derrick between boat and bank.

culprits were usually charged the cost of the repairs, although a good record could lessen a penalty. Sometimes bridges were either lowered too soon or not raised quickly enough and so claims that it had to be the boat's fault—because it was moving and the structure was stationary—were not always true.

The Forth & Clyde's bridges were designed to be worked by two people, one on either side of the canal. The company's bridge keeper operated the offside leaf, while the boat operator had to open and close the towpath side. In the days of horse-drawn vessels this was done by the tracker, who was already on the path, but the crews of powered boats had a problem. The lightermen solved it by having one of them—usually the mate—hang on the end of the derrick and swing out over the water and on to the towpath. It was a practice that would give today's health and safety legislators apoplexy, but it kept the boat moving in centre channel and did not risk losing time or damaging the boat by bringing her alongside. The same practice was employed at locks to speed the boat's passage. Other vessels, like fishing boats and yachts, kept a bicycle on board and one of the crew worked their passage the hard way!

Scows or lighters loaded with coal often lay uncovered and unattended in Kirkintilloch's Hillhead Basin, and few left with their cargoes intact. Many local people stocked up on free coal—no doubt alerted by a grapevine that had something to do with the fact that the boatmen also lived in Hillhead! Colliery-owners William Baird & Sons lost a lot in transit between Twechar Colliery and Dawsholm Gasworks at Maryhill; an average of one ton a day went astray in November 1898! Baird's lighter *Closeburn* was raided frequently, but other boats were hit too. In 1904 two boatmen from Grangemouth simply tied up alongside Baird's scow *Kennowart* and replenished their bunkers from her cargo. Acting on a tip-off in March 1898, a policeman found fifteen children stripping the scow *Nora*. He gave chase and managed to catch one girl who had so much coal gathered in her apron she could hardly move! Perhaps the constable needed some fitness training![10]

Kirkintilloch's Hillhead Basin, where the cargoes of coal scows were regularly raided.

Lightermen saw themselves as an elite, although there was nothing romantic about being a canal boatman. The average lighter was usually operated by a crew of three: skipper, mate and engineer. When they were away from home they shared a tiny cabin with an iron stove as heater and cooker, and each man had a six foot by three foot bunk and a small locker for personal possessions. These prosaic boats were not the decorated barges of English canals; they were not homes, but places of work, and work could be seventeen hours or more a day, even in the dark and fog of winter. Most boats ran between Grangemouth docks and Glasgow and a good, sober skipper, who had served a long apprenticeship and knew the road, could be relied on to make the passage as close to time as the canal would allow.[11]

The men had little respite from a hard, poorly paid, itinerant life which gave them little time with their families. To relieve some of the social deficit, a mission and institute for canal boatmen was established at Port Dundas in 1870. It aimed 'to promote the social, moral and religious welfare of Canal Boatmen . . . and their families'. Charles Rennie Mackintosh is thought to have had a hand in the design of the building which contained a large mission hall, used for regular services and other activities like the Boy's Brigade, Band of Hope and the Port Dundas Pleasant Sunday Afternoon Society! Small services were also held on board boats.[12]

Caretakers Mr and Mrs Leslie and two unidentified women on the steps of the Canal Boatmen's Institute and Port Dundas Mission.

The steam lighter *Comet* going east through Lock 15, Camelon.

A steam lighter at Lock 16, Camelon, c.1905.

A new union, the Boatmen and Labourers Forth & Clyde Navigation Association, was formed in April 1904 and by mid-September it was on strike. The men sought higher wages, claiming these had stagnated while trade had increased. They also sought proper sanitary conditions in the scows, a claim ridiculed by the companies on the basis that the men made a mess of the boats themselves. The dispute turned ugly and boats worked by non-union men were pelted with stones as they passed places where the strike had strong support. Police had to escort those boats which were still operating through hot-spots like Kirkintilloch Hillhead and Port Dundas. Men working two scows were attacked near Cadder by strikers from a Carron Company boat. Some 'blacklegs' were beaten up and one, 'Mad Harry', a simple unwordly man who had been taken on by the Kirkintilloch firm of J. & J. Hay, was found fatally injured in a scow at Port Dundas. The strike lasted for six weeks with J. & J. Hay resisting the men's demands longer than the other companies.[13]

Some men did not live up to others' high standards. The skipper of William Jack & Co.'s *Basuto* appeared at Falkirk Sheriff Court in 1907 after a drunken confrontation with a lock. He drove into the gates, bounced back into the gates at his stern, and rebounded into the first gates. Having got into the lock he and the mate started a drink-fuelled fight and the lock keeper, fearing for the canal, asked the skipper to remove his vessel and go no further. He refused, blocking the canal for half an hour and delaying Salvesen & Co.'s *Comet* which was waiting to enter the lock.[14]

Lightermen regarded the men who worked the horse-drawn scows as the lowest form of canal life: drunken, worthless and not to be trusted on a steam boat for fear they would steal the engine! It was a tough life which many did indeed combine with hard drink and strong language, as the skipper of the Falkirk-based lighter *Nellie* discovered in May 1892. Two half-drunk men working William Jack's scow No. 7 arrived at Hillhead Basin at 2 p.m. They moored up, fed the horse and took another wee refreshment themselves. Two hours later the bridge keeper stopped them from setting off, but at 9 p.m. they got under way. A short while later the *Nellie* followed them through Hillhead Bridge. It was dark as she approached Tintock, but luckily the skipper saw the unlit shape of No. 7 lying across the canal and managed to stop before crashing into her. He and his crew boarded the scow and found the two men asleep in their cabin, so drunk that one had his arm on the lighted stove. Neither heard anything until they were shaken from their slumbers.[15]

Nellie and *Annie* ran a regular service between Falkirk and Glasgow. Traders in the town had a system whereby they ordered goods by placing envelopes in their window for Turnbull, the local carrier, to pick up. He delivered these to the skipper who took them to Port Dundas and gave them to another carter in the city who collected the goods and brought them to the boat. They were delivered to the businesses in Falkirk the following day, a speed of service that railways apparently never matched!

Canal boatmen were noted for the kind of quirky humour immortalised in the *Para Handy* stories, as in this fragment of a late nineteenth century music-hall song, *The Voyage of the Mary Jane, of Grangemouth*:

> Oh, I'll sing to you of a ship and crew,
> Of bricks we had a load,
> On a voyage of discovery boys,
> We sailed up the Maryhill Road.

Lambhill Bridge

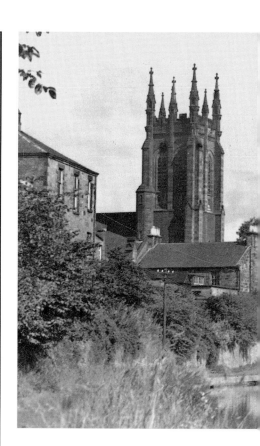

blether at the bridge

Balmore Road in Glasgow was closed for about seven hours in 1955 when a puffer loaded with cables ran aground at Lambhill Bridge. The bridge could not be lowered and so, while the puffer remained stuck in the mud, people wanting to cross the canal had to walk over the boat by means of a couple of ladders.[4]

rth and Clyde Canal, Falkirk.

Kirkintilloch twilight: lighters alongside Hay's yard in the last years of the canal.

When crossing by the public park,
 A wave swept o'er our deck,
Which washed the captain overboard,
 With the anchor round his neck.
Our provisions being exhausted, we
 had nothing to feed upon,
When the purser sent the mate ashore
 For a ha'penny sweet milk scone;
But as the bakers' shops were shut,
 With pain we commenced to holler,
When one of the crew, in a fit of despair,
 He guzzled the horse's collar.
When sailing round by Tintock Tap
 The weather was so severe,
That for the space of a hundred weeks
 We neither could see nor hear.
Then the Captain sent a man aloft
 To see what could be done,
But the feet were burned out of his socks
 By the heat of the scorching sun.
Thus we sailed and sailed on the tragic main
 'Till we could sail no more,
Then the Captain gave us a bar of soap,
 And we washed ourselves ashore.

Another fragment of a similar song has also survived:

'The sea! the sea! is the life for me,'
As our Captain used to bawl,
When we steered away for foreign parts,
On the Forth & Clyde Canaul.
We had not gone for many days
When a fearful storm arose;
The mate threw off his big top coat,
And up aloft he goes.
He cried, "The ship is going down,
Or else she's off her course;"
He told a man to jump ashore
And try to stop the horse.

Horses had a hard life too. Some fell in the canal and not all got out; others were abused and made to work when unfit or injured. Handlers sometimes rode on them, or if drunk and tired let the horse lead the way while they held on to its tail. Penalties for mistreating horses were often small, as in 1895 when a boatman was fined a few shillings for beating a frightened horse which had fallen in the canal at Cadder. The incident inspired angry letters to the *Kirkintilloch Herald*, but the paper was able to praise boatyard workers in 1906 when a horse was literally propelled into the canal when its raft of timber stopped suddenly, breaking the rope. The men persuaded the animal to swim through Townhead Bridge and climb out at the launching slip. They saved another horse in 1912 by attaching a rope to its collar and steering it ashore at the slip.[16]

Romantic Forth & Clyde: a steam lighter at Falkirk.

Taking a stroll at Drumshoreland near Broxburn.
West Lothian Libraries; Broxburn Academy Collection.

A typical canal barge trip at Coatbridge on the Monkland Canal.

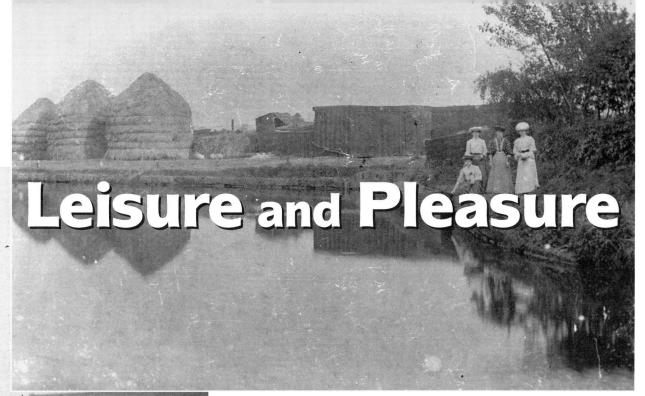

Leisure and Pleasure

In the days when people had little time or money for a holiday, a day out on a cleaned-up scow was quite a treat. One such trip left Port Dundas in drizzling rain in the 1870s with youngsters cramming the hold, their merry faces peeping out over the bulwarks in joyful anticipation of what lay ahead. The writer who watched them leave later saw the boat at the side of the canal while the children ran races and played football in a field.[1]

All sorts of organisations including Sunday schools, temperance associations and political parties went for such outings and excursions. In 1890 coal and iron trade salesmen journeyed on the lighter *Albert* from Port Dundas to Kirkintilloch where they lunched in the loft of J. & J. Hay's boatyard. In the afternoon they sailed on to Wyndford and returned to Glasgow by train. The Springburn Corps of the Salvation Army went out to Kirkintilloch on the scow *David* in June 1901. They were towed by a former tramway horse doing its first day's duty on the towpath. It kept stopping, perhaps because it expected passengers to get on and off, but more likely because it couldn't resist munching the grass verges having been used to barren cobbled streets. Eventually the boat arrived at a field where the passengers enjoyed games and refreshments before returning to the city.[2]

Some trips did not go according to plan. In August 1901, 1,000 people gathered at Townhead Bridge for the Kirkintilloch Conservative Association's annual excursion and picnic at Cadder. Waiting for them, decorated with flags and bunting, were four scows and the lighter *Moor*. She was clearly the favourite boat and over 300 people crowded aboard, along with the Rechabite Band. With so many people on deck, the unballasted lighter was top heavy and started to roll as soon as she cast off. Initially she stayed against the bank, but as the roll increased, the band (who were some years too early to have the example of the *Titanic's* band to follow!) stopped playing. Frightened people leapt ashore causing the *Moor* to slew across the canal into the path of an oncoming scow. It

Edinburgh University's boathouse, 1909.

Union Canal, near Summerford.   *Falkirk.*

There were boat-hirers on the Union Canal at Falkirk where rowing and romancing were popular pastimes.

also had passengers aboard and as it headed for the bank they jumped ashore, except for one woman who fell into the water! The *Moor* was brought back alongside. Some passengers went home in distress, others boarded the scows and some intrepid souls stayed on the lighter. They all eventually got to Cadder to enjoy refreshments, music and a variety of races, including one for the boatmen.[3]

Taking a boat trip for the fun of it had a long pedigree on the Union Canal where the original Canal Company operated light pleasure boats. Three trips a day went from Port Hopetoun to Slateford, Ratho and the Almond Aqueduct where people could buy refreshments, fruit and confectionery before the return journey. Such rarefied pleasures had receded into canal history by the 1900s when children dressed in bright frocks and Eton collars, their knees scrubbed clean and with tinnies hung round their necks on strings, crowded onto scows for trips into the country. Sometimes a candy-striped awning protected the occupants. Vellore Farm at Muiravonside and Carribber Glen were popular destinations for boats from Linlithgow and elsewhere, while boats from Edinburgh went to Ratho. They were operated by John Johnstone who started a boat hiring business in 1906 at Lochrin Basin.

An Edinburgh amateur opera company took an annual trip. They started by hoisting a piano on board and set off, taking what cover they could from words and worse hurled by urban urchins from city bridges. Verbal abuse, tame by modern standards, included such gems as 'had a rough voyage' or 'got a parrot on board'. If it was raining, the boat stopped under Ratho Bridge, but the bargeman usually sheltered in one of the village's many pubs. Returning home on one occasion, and distracted by an urgent drink-induced call of nature, he was knocked overboard by the tiller. Amid much hilarity his passengers hauled him back on board, although history does not record if the drama was played out to piano accompaniment. On another occasion when the bargeman had imbibed too freely he started the return trip by wandering into the canal followed by his faithful horse.[4]

Private boating developed strongly on the Union Canal, perhaps encouraged by the small amount of commercial traffic. The North British Railway Company issued licences and published notices to regulate the use of private boats, a small number of which appear to have been powered by steam or electricity. A special electric boat service ran between Fountainbridge and the Edinburgh International Exhibition of Electrical Engineering, General Invention and Industries at Meggetland in 1890. There were four launches operated by the General Electric Power and Traction Company Ltd. and they ran at 45 minute intervals with extra services in the last two hours. People could buy an inclusive ticket for the trip and admission to the site, take the trip on its own at a reduced cost, or go on a special trip to Ratho. Another feature of the exhibition was the 'ship railway' which was set up between the Ashley Terrace and Meggetland Bridges. Boats were drawn out of the water on a railway line which looped round the site before returning to the canal. Despite these attractions, bad weather deterred the crowds and the exhibition was a flop.

Rowing, as a competition sport, began in 1846 when the first organised club, the St Andrew Boat Club, was founded at Meggetland in Edinburgh. Other groups, including some of the big city schools and Edinburgh University, followed, and the sport became one the most enduring activities on either canal.

Ordinary rowing boats were also popular. Some were privately owned,

Although the attempt to customise this postcard for Broxburn has missed, it encapsulates the Union Canal's romantic attractions. The view of the scow crossing the Almond Aqueduct was clearly taken seconds before the one on page 72.

Steam launch at Redding.

Falkirk Museums; Callendar House.

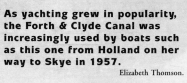

As yachting grew in popularity, the Forth & Clyde Canal was increasingly used by boats such as this one from Holland on her way to Skye in 1957.

Elizabeth Thomson.

A picnic by the Forth & Clyde near Auchinstarry.

Elizabeth Thomson.

Mariner's Day at Lock 16, Camelon, in the 1950s.

Margaret Heriot.

Canoeing on the Union Canal at Bantaskine Bridge, 1935.

A family outing by the Union Canal near Slateford.

Crown Copyright: Royal Commission on the Ancient and Historical Monuments of Scotland (Chrystal Collection).

Fishing by the Union Canal locks, Falkirk.

Falkirk Museums; Callendar House.

Great Broxburn icicle

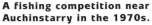

A fishing competition near Auchinstarry in the 1970s.

while others, like those of John Johnstone at Lochrin Basin, were available for hire. The boathouse, decorated in later years with a mural of the Loch Ness monster, was the stuff of childhood dreams—or nightmares—while the boats themselves offered those a wee bit older the chance to fantasise. Young men splashed about, ever hopeful their antics would impress the girls but not incur the boatmaster's wrath and earn a ban which would curtail such courtship displays. A boat could be had for an hour, three hours, or a day, depending on the price, but the real challenge was to take the three hour stint and row to Meggetland and back and, if possible, pick up some desirable company on the way. The good boats were numbers one, four, six, seven and ten, although number six, a sleek greyhound, was best, while numbers two, five, eight and nine were slow and unimpressive, and three had a dodgy rowlock. In later years there were kayaks for individuals who wanted speed and the chance to explore, but it needed experience to stay dry in one of these boats. The boats continued to attract customers into the 1960s, when the business was operated by a Mrs Beak and the boats had names instead of numbers.[5]

In June 1922 a Miss Foy F. Quiller-Couch was logged passing Lock 16 in a rowing boat on her way to Glasgow. She was presumably Foy Felicia, the daughter of the writer Sir Arthur Quiller-Couch, or Q as he was known, and was regarded as a good oarswoman. But was she rowing from Edinburgh to Glasgow or just from Falkirk, and why was she doing it? We will probably never know.[6]

The Girls' Nautical Training Corps briefly set up a base in an old university boathouse at Harrison Bridge and raised sufficient funds to launch a rowing boat, the *Venture*, and a canoe, the *Venturesome*, in 1952. The canal was ideal for canoeing which became popular with schools, cadet corps, organised clubs and individuals.[7]

There were many other leisure pursuits on the canals. Walking was popular, especially along the Union Canal and in particular in the Falkirk area where the Bantaskine parkland to the south, and views of the hills to the north, made it an attractive setting. The same section of canal was used by skaters in winter. Curlers also used the canals for matches at Linlithgow, Port Downie, Camelon, on the Grangemouth timber basins and at Wyndford. The spectacle of the 'Great Broxburn Icicle' became an attraction for winter walkers in 1895 when the overflow from the Almond Aqueduct froze down to the river, 76 feet below.

Many people learned to swim in the canals, including at least one Scottish junior champion, Roddy MacRitchie, whose climb up the sporting ladder started in the water beside the White House pub at Maryhill. The basins between the Union Canal locks at Falkirk were a favourite spot with the lock gates making an ideal platform for jumping off into the water, ten feet below.

Fishing has always been popular with a range of enthusiasts from the serious angler to small children with a jeely jar catching minnows, beardies and soldiers—attractive little fish with a red blotch on their backs.[8] Species like pike, perch and roach were most common, but as well as providing a habitat for the unusual leather carp, the Union Canal could also boast the occasional brown trout brought down by the Almond feeder. In later years the Forth & Clyde became a popular competition venue for coarse anglers, with bus-loads of people travelling from the North of England to take part. The canal's deterioration after closure saw this activity fade while informal fishing carried on.

Fairy Queen (1).

Gipsy Queen leaving Port Dundas with a hearty load!

The Queens

Parents and children on the *Gipsy Queen*.

The little passenger steamer *Rockvilla Castle*, which replaced the horse-drawn swifts on the Forth & Clyde in 1859, was taken over in 1875 by a George Aitken of Kirkintilloch. He operated her on regular services and a variety of pleasure trips until he was tragically drowned in 1880. Another company took the vessel over, but after only a year she was withdrawn and broken up. More than ten years went by during which the only pleasure craft on the canal were cleaned up scows or lighters, but in 1893 James Aitken, the son of *Rockvilla Castle*'s former owner, put a little steamer called *Fairy Queen* into service.

For the first two seasons the boat and her crew worked a punishing schedule. They went from Kirkintilloch to Port Dundas in the morning and from there made two return trips to Craigmarloch, before returning to Kirkintilloch about fourteen hours after they had started. By 1896 the venture had become established and the itinerary was modified, but the steamer was too small and so James Aitken sold *Fairy Queen* in 1897 and replaced her with a new boat of the same name. Demand soon outstripped this larger steamer's capacity and in May 1903 a new vessel, *May Queen*, was launched from the Kirkintilloch boatyard of Peter McGregor & Son, the only one of the little fleet to have been built on the canal (the first *Fairy Queen* had been built at Irvine and the second at Paisley). *May Queen* and *Fairy Queen* (2) sailed between Kirkintilloch, Port Dundas and Craigmarloch, with the occasional extended tour, but again demand outstripped supply and in May 1905 James Aitken took delivery of a new boat, *Gipsy Queen*, from the Paisley yard of Bow, McLachlan & Company. She was the largest vessel ever to sail on the canal and on 10 May 1905 she went from Kirkintilloch to Craigmarloch where new facilities had been created. There was a bungalow with a dining hall and veranda on the ground floor, and a tearoom and balcony upstairs. Outside there was a park with a putting green and swings, and moored in the basin a scow called *Meadow Queen*, with a private tearoom and dancing deck. In twelve years James Aitken had built up from one small steamer to a fleet of three, created a mini-resort as a destination, and seen off competition from another steamer, *Truro Belle*, which only lasted for one season. If the boats were Queens, he was the King!

He was also unsentimental and in 1911 sold *Fairy Queen* (2) to a Tyneside shipbuilder who painted her hull black and took her through the canal to the east coast. *May Queen* followed her to the Tyne in 1918.[9]

Gipsy Queen continued to ply from Port Dundas to Craigmarloch. There was a tearoom on board and a band which played while passengers enjoyed impromptu ceilidhs. Children ran alongside, performing antics in the hope that passengers would reward them by throwing coins. To some people this was harmless fun, but to those who had to look after children's welfare and education it was an activity that placed them in danger of falling in the water and took them away from school.[10]

A small motor boat, *Fairy Queen* (3), was put on in 1923. She took trips from Craigmarloch to Wyndford and could get people back to the city faster than *Gipsy Queen*, but she was an unremarkable little boat and with no tearoom or dancing space was never very popular. She did however feature in a gramophone record made by Bob Smith and his Ideal Band. It was made for Beltona Records of Glasgow at the Edison Bell Studios in Peckham, London, in April 1929 and was entitled *The Canal Cruise*. It was a heady mix of music and back-chat from the band and included a solo by Tony Capaldi, a popular

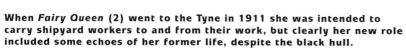

May Queen at
Kirkintilloch.

A romantic postcard of
Fairy Queen (2) near
Craigmarloch Woods.

When *Fairy Queen* (2) went to the Tyne in 1911 she was intended to
carry shipyard workers to and from their work, but clearly her new role
included some echoes of her former life, despite the black hull.

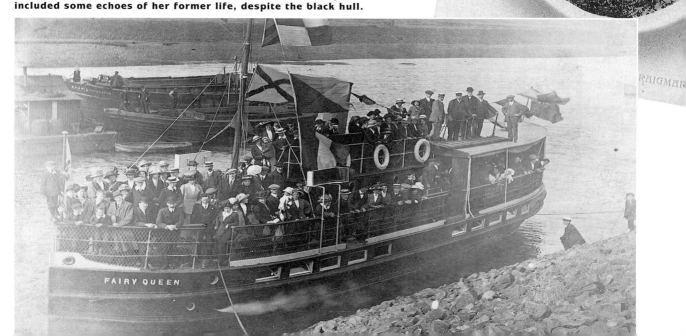

The Craigmarloch bungalow at three different stages of development.

Inside the bungalow.
East Dunbartonshire Libraries: The William Patrick Library, Kirkintilloch.

Boating at Craigmarloch.

Putting at Craigmarloch.

Malcolm Stark, skipper of *Gipsy Queen* from 1929 to 1940.

Italian accordion-playing café owner from Parkhead. There was also a song by Charles Knight who later went solo as 'Glasgow's Tramway Tenor':

When you want to forget for an hour or two,
The troubles, the trials that are troubling you,
Just promise yourself a change of scene,
And book your fare on the *Fairy Queen*.
And sail away, at the close of day,
On the Forth & Clyde Canal,
In the rustling trees, in the summer breeze,
On the Forth & Canal.
Join in the fun, with everyone
And prove yourself a pal,
On the brand new ship, on the brand new trip,
On the Forth & Clyde Canal.

A second Canal Cruise record featured *Gipsy Queen*.

The tradition of cargo lighters taking excursions carried on in the Falkirk area into the 1920s, although the steamers did venture east on occasions. The Falkirk Burgh Merchants Association, with the Falkirk District Grocers Association, chartered *Gipsy Queen* for annual excursions. These took place at the end of June on a Wednesday, the burgh's early closing day, and when the shops shut, traders and shop girls alike set off in high spirits to join the boat at Lock 16. She left at 2 p.m. and after high tea at Craigmarloch set sail for Kirkintilloch where she turned, and with music, a concert and dancing to entertain the passengers, headed back to Falkirk, arriving at 9.30 p.m.[11]

James Aitken died in 1930 and his son George took over, just as the lean Depression years and the advance of road transport took their toll on customer numbers. There was a small revival in 1939 as the clouds of war gathered and people sensed that life was about to change, but the war, when it came, brought *Gipsy Queen*'s season to an end. She was laid up at Craigmarloch for the winter and in June 1940 was towed to Bowling by a couple of horses. From there she was taken to the breaker's yard and a little bit of Scotland's folk culture died.[12]

A watery encounter for a pug locomotive at Redding.
Falkirk Museums; Callendar House.

Opposite: **Dilapidation on the Union Canal in Edinburgh in the 1920s.**
Crown Copyright: Royal Commission on the Ancient and Historical Monuments of Scotland (Chrystal Collection).

Below left: **Swing bridge on the Orchard Hall Branch before demolition to make way for the Falkirk distributor road.**

Below: **Kilpunt Bridge on the Union Canal with the Edinburgh to Bathgate railway bridge beyond.**
West Lothian Libraries; Broxburn Academy Collection.

The Long Decline

Rails and Roads

As railways expanded through the nineteenth century they not only took away the canals' industrial markets, but also interrupted their operations while bridges and tunnels were being built. These changed the look of the canals too.

The Union Canal was easier for railways to cross, although fewer lines did it. Tracks were extended from the Causewayend transshipment basin across the canal to join up with the Edinburgh & Glasgow Railway at Manuel and its Bo'ness Branch. The Edinburgh to Bathgate railway, which opened in 1850, crossed the canal between Broxburn and Ratho. The Caledonian Railway opened their route from Glasgow Central through Carstairs to Edinburgh in 1848. It crossed the Water of Leith beside Slateford Aqueduct on a splendid viaduct and then carried on over the canal just east of Kingsknowe station. Another bridge, further to the east, took the Balerno Branch, opened in 1874, back over the canal. The Edinburgh Suburban & Southside Junction Railway opened in 1884, with an impressive tunnel under the canal north of Craiglockhart station. Elsewhere bridges carried industrial branch lines across the water to Broxburn oilworks, and Callendar Colliery and brickworks at Falkirk. A colliery hutch road crossed the canal at South Bantaskine and simple swing bridges served the explosives works and colliery at Redding.

The greater depth of the Forth & Clyde and the need to maintain clear headroom for masted vessels made it more difficult for the railways to cross, but the Scottish Central Railway, which opened in 1848, tunnelled under it at Carmuirs. In the same year the Campsie Branch Railway neatly avoided the problem by utilising the arch of the Luggie Aqueduct. Later, the Kelvin Aqueduct was also used as a ready-made route under the canal.

In the Glasgow area the main lines into Queen Street and Buchanan Street stations tunnelled under Port Dundas. The single-track Glasgow, Dumbarton & Helensburgh Railway went under the canal near Lambhill in 1858 and, when the track was doubled and the tunnel widened in 1900, the

Tram on Falkirk's 'Circular' route crossing Bainsford Bridge.

Expansion of Grangemouth Docks c.1905 with the River Carron running past the docks on the left.

Maryhill Road Aqueduct.

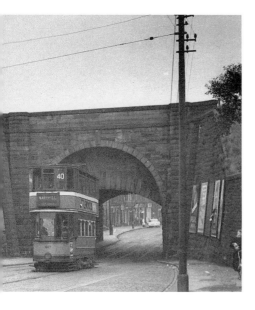

Tram on Colinton Road near Meggetland Bridge.

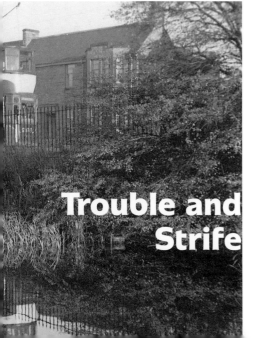

Trouble and Strife

aqueduct known officially as Hillend Bridge and locally as Hallowe'en Pend was altered to accommodate it. The canal above Lock 26 at Temple was diverted for eighteen months in 1871/72 while a tunnel was made for the Stobcross Railway, and in 1884 the Knightswood Tunnel was made between Locks 26 and 27. It was built in a cutting with masonry-lined walls and a roof of cast iron girders, topped with concrete and clay puddle. Navigation was maintained across the excavation by a huge iron caisson, but when it was floated away the puddling failed and water flooded the tunnel to a depth of ten feet. The canal had to be drained to carry out repairs.[1]

Other tunnels were made in the 1890s on the Glasgow, Yoker & Clydebank Railway at Dalmuir and the Glasgow Central Railway's extension from Maryhill Central to Possil. A tunnel was also made to connect Dawsholm and Temple gasworks.

Swing bridges were often remarkable pieces of engineering although they mostly served only sidings, factories, or mines. There were two at Bowling, one an impressive structure dating from 1896 for the Caledonian Railway from Dumbarton and the other, a simple bridge, for goods traffic at the lower basin. Freight trains used a splendid bridge at Singer's Clydebank works and two simpler ones across the Port Dundas basins to Spiers Wharf. Other simple swing bridges were made for colliery railways at Mavis Valley and Twechar, and access into Lochburn Ironworks near Lambhill. A fine bridge on the Orchard Hall Branch between Falkirk and Grangemouth was scrapped to build a new road, but main line trains still cross the now fixed and immovable bridge at Lock 9, to the west of Falkirk Grahamston station.

The proximity of so many railways was also, paradoxically, a source of canal revenue, because canal water was piped to the tracksides for the use of steam locomotives. The railway owners of each canal were even happy to supply water to rival companies—at a price!

Improvements to road transport started to affect the Forth & Clyde Canal before the end of the nineteenth century. In Glasgow three aqueducts were built around 1880 to allow the city's tramway system to expand. One was for a new road, Bilsland Drive, but the others, at Possil Road and Maryhill Road, were replacements for small original aqueducts. At Possil Road the old structure remained in place and the road was realigned through the new one, but problems arose at Maryhill. The intention was to demolish the old structure on completion of the new one which was built immediately alongside, on the city side of the road. The canal had to be taken through a much sharper S-bend to cross it and it also gobbled up a chunk of the neighbouring Gairbraid Church's ground. Work was well advanced in April 1882 when a coffer dam gave way, flooding the road and much of the surrounding area. Stop planks had to be rapidly put in at Lambhill and Ruchill Bridges, and the water run off to prevent the embankment collapsing and thereby causing a major catastrophe.[2]

At Falkirk, swing bridges were built in 1905 to replace the old Camelon and Bainsford Bridges so that tramcars on the new 'Circular' route could cross the canal, and at Clydebank tram-carrying swing bridges replaced bascule bridges at Dalmuir in February 1915 and Kilbowie Road a year later.[3]

Canal mania swept Britain again in the last two decades of the nineteenth century. The hot topic was the Manchester Ship Canal, but while that idea quickly became a reality proposals to make a ship canal across central Scotland never

The Daily Mirror

THE MORNING JOURNAL WITH THE SECOND LARGEST NET SALE.

One Halfpenny.

WEDNESDAY, JANUARY 8, 1913

2,873.   Registered at the G.P.O. as a Newspaper.

PIERCING SCOTLAND BY CANAL: TWO SCHEMES FOR LINKING THE NORTH SEA TO THE ATLANTIC OCEAN.

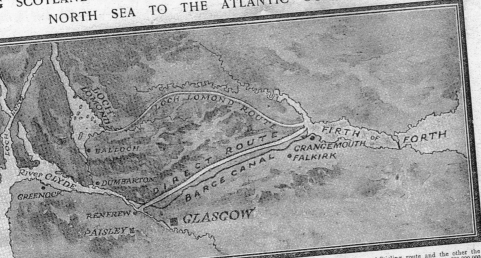

Two schemes for a canal through Scotland, which is regarded in Edinburgh and Glasgow as the inevitable crowning work to the establishment of the naval base at Rosyth, have now been put forward. As shown in the above map, one scheme would follow what is called the Loch Lomond-Stirling route and the other the direct route parallel with the old barge canal. The former would cost £20,000,000 and the latter £24,000,000. Full and interesting particulars appear on page 4.

NEWS PORTRAITS.

Mr. Tom Taylor, Bolton's new M.P., who has made a successful maiden speech. "Though I may never speak, I can vote," he said before election.

Mr. James Patten, one of those who are being tried in connection with the cotton "corner" in New York.

FUNERAL SHIP BADLY DAMAGED BY STORM WHILE CROSSING THE ATLANTIC.

OBITUARY.

Capt. Hjalmar Johansen, the Arctic explorer, who was found dead in

The ship canal that never was.

A canal trip on *Gipsy Queen* for wounded World War I servicemen.

Semple Street Bridge with Port Hopetoun drained.
Crown Copyright: Royal Commission on the Ancient and Historical Monuments of Scotland (Chrystal Collection).

The First World War

Laying the World War I oil pipeline through Maryhill.
City of Glasgow Libraries and Archives; The Mitchell Library.

got beyond the drawing board or the letters columns of newspapers. Plans presented in the 1880s, before and during the First World War and again into the 1930s generated interest but no action. The protracted debate damaged the way people viewed the Forth & Clyde Canal, because those pushing the ship canal found it expedient to dismiss the 'barge canal' as worthless. The mud stuck and the country's failure to upgrade the old canal to ship canal status was used as a convenient stick to beat it with right up to the 1960s.

Much of the debate over the ship canal centred on its value to the Navy at times when conflict of one sort or another never seemed far below the surface. In January 1883, during the Fenian troubles, a bomb exploded on Possil Road Aqueduct. It injured some people although the intention may have been to burst the canal and flood Glasgow.[4] A spate of 'incendiarism' at Glasgow sawmills in the autumn of 1908 may also have had a political motive. Of those fires beside the canal, one at the Western Sawmill, Firhill, was followed less than two weeks later by a serious blaze at Temple Sawmills.[5]

Traffic dwindled on the Union Canal in the early years of the twentieth century and the Falkirk lock flight was used less and less. Only the occasional scow came down to the Falkirk area with road metal or rubble stone, although a launch was delivered in 1913 from Port Dundas to John Johnstone's boat hiring business at Lochrin Basin.[6] Just round the corner from there, Port Hopetoun and Port Hamilton had deteriorated to the extent that they could have challenged Jack the Ripper's Whitechapel as Britain's most melodramatic setting. The Stygian deserted basins were often drained to search for evidence of crime, while decades of decline had turned the dilapidated soot-blackened buildings into the city's worst slum. The area's clearance was approved by Edinburgh Corporation in 1912, but delayed by the outbreak of the First World War.[7]

Every 24 hours before the war 40 or 50 boats passed between Grangemouth and Port Dundas, but when hostilities began the Admiralty closed the Firth of Forth to commercial shipping, cutting off Grangemouth from the outside world. The impact on the canal was severe: the Leith, Hull & Hamburg Steam Packet Co.'s twelve boats trading with Germany were stopped; the Carron Company's five boats trading with Germany were taken off; Rankin & Co. of Glasgow, who traded with Rotterdam, took off their eight lighters; J. & J. Hay stopped their six steamers and twenty scows; William Jack & Co. laid up five steamers and ten scows and Salvesen & Co. of Grangemouth suspended eight lighters! Some redundant lighters were requisitioned by the Admiralty to act as North Sea fleet tenders, but their canal days were over. Internal movement and west-coast trade continued, and the opportunity was taken to carry out repairs and dredging, but the bustle had gone.[8]

Cadets associated with the North British Rubber Co. parading beside Lochrin Basin, 1919.

Leamington Bridge at Fountainbridge before its removal to Gilmore Park.

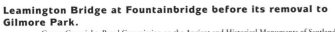

Crown Copyright: Royal Commission on the Ancient and Historical Monuments of Scotland (Chrystal Collection).

Bustle came suddenly to Dalmuir one August evening in 1916. A young man walking along the towpath near Trafalgar Street noticed water trickling through the canal bank. He informed the police, but before they could do anything the bank had been breached and the trickle had turned into a torrent pouring down Trafalgar Street and Buchanan Street to Dumbarton Road. People were shocked to see the placid canal transformed into an angry brown spate raging through their closes. The gates of Beardmore's shipyard were opened to give the water a route to the Clyde, but it flooded the yard instead. Buildings were also inundated, but no serious damage or loss of life occurred. The locks further up the canal were closed and eventually the water dissipated, leaving enormous puddles for children to play in.[9]

There was more feverish activity in 1918 when the Admiralty laid a pipeline under the towpath from their oil terminal on the Clyde at Old Kilpatrick to Grangemouth docks. From there the oil was to be shipped across the Forth to Rosyth Naval Base. Intermediate pumping stations were set up at Hungryside and Castlecary. A team of specialist American pipe-layers, assisted by local contractors and two companies of Royal Marines Engineers, carried out the work. They started on 11 July and the first oil was pumped into the Grangemouth tanks on 9 November—two days before the war ended![10]

Below: **Lothian House, built on the site of Port Hopetoun in the 1930s and the carved frieze on the facade.**

Between the Wars

The restrictions on shipping in the Forth were lifted in January 1919, but the *Kirkintilloch Herald*'s confident predictions that scows would soon be a familiar sight again were not fulfilled. The trade had gone and the Forth & Clyde's long decline had begun.[11]

The end came for Port Hopetoun and Port Hamilton when Edinburgh Corporation purchased them in 1922. The basins were filled in and a new terminal was created at Lochrin Basin. The distinctive canalside structures, including the old Hopetoun House on the corner of Semple and Morrison Streets where the port manager had once lived, were demolished. The remarkable Leamington Lift Bridge, which had been erected early in the twentieth century at Fountainbridge, was removed to Gilmore Park. A bakery was built where Port Hamilton had been and a large tax office, Lothian House, was erected in 1935/36 on the site of Port Hopetoun. The old basin was commemorated on the building's facade by a stone carving of a canal barge, but there is a second canal connection: the cast iron panels in the window recesses were made at the Lion Foundry in Kirkintilloch.

As a result of railway company amalgamations in 1926, ownership of the Union Canal passed to the London & North Eastern Railway (LNER) and the London, Midland & Scottish Railway (LMS) took over the Forth & Clyde. But it was now roads, not railways, that posed the biggest threat to the canals.

Motor vehicle numbers increased rapidly after the war and the old wooden bridges on the Forth & Clyde were seen as obstacles to progress. Castlecary Bridge on the Glasgow to Stirling Road was an early target for criticism, particularly in 1925 when a steam wagon crashed through it and traffic had to be diverted through Kilsyth and over the equally flimsy Glasgow Road Bridge. Stirling County Council sought financial assistance from other local authorities who might benefit from a new bridge, but were rebuffed and had to go ahead with only a 50 per cent grant from the Ministry of Transport. Lanarkshire County Council also had to make do with a 50 per cent Government grant after Kilsyth and Kirkintilloch Town Councils refused to help with a replacement

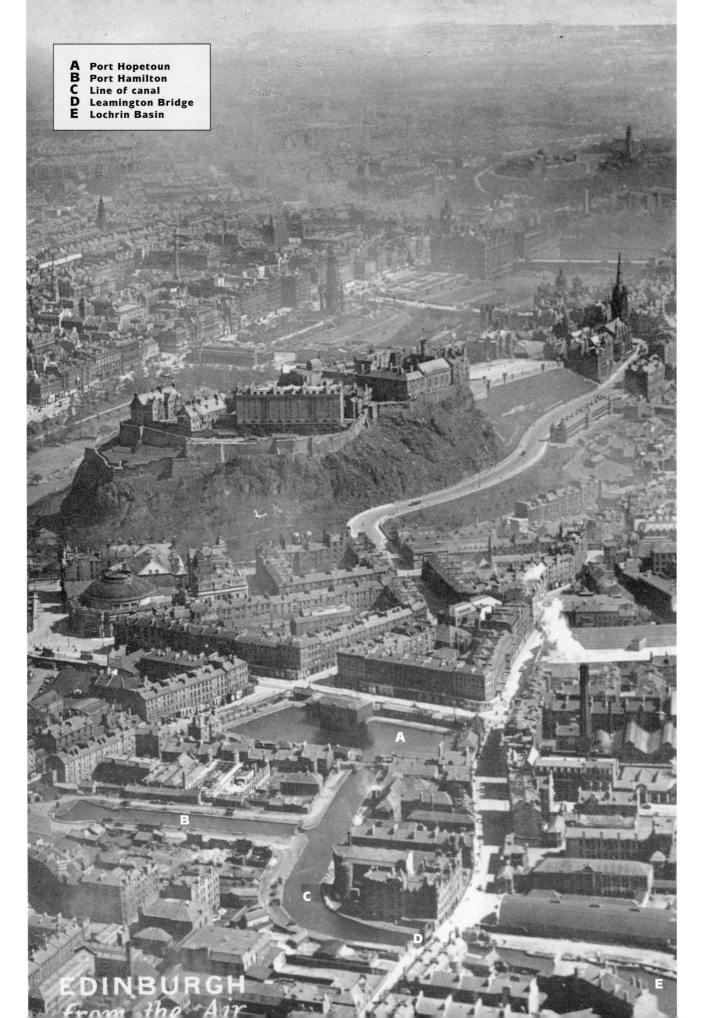

A Port Hopetoun
B Port Hamilton
C Line of canal
D Leamington Bridge
E Lochrin Basin

EDINBURGH
from the Air

for Glasgow Road Bridge. The contractors, Sir William Arrol & Co., began work at Castlecary in September 1927 and at Glasgow Road Bridge a few weeks later. The bridges were operational early the following year.[12]

While Glasgow Road Bridge was being rebuilt, traffic had to go round by Torrance. Buses struggled on the wet, slippery roads and three collided at Hungryside Bridge early in 1928. Kirkintilloch and Kilsyth got little sympathy from Lanarkshire County Council which seemed to regard the inconvenience as the price the towns had to pay for not contributing to the cost.

As soon as work started on these two bridges, the debate about others became more voluble. It was particularly loud in Kirkintilloch where Townhead Bridge linked the two sides of the town centre. Calls for a replacement had rumbled on for years and in 1921, when the old bridge had to be closed for repairs, some unkind things were said about it. A contributor to the *Kirkintilloch Herald* put them in verse:

> O Toonheid Brig, O Toonheid Brig,
> I think you've served your day;
> Auld age is creeping ower ye noo,
> Yer 'dinness' ye display.
> Ye aince were muckle thocht o',
> But noo that day is past,
> An' though ye're noo baith auld and frail,
> Yer end's no coming fast.

'The Auld Brig' itself replied:

> An' noo I'm telt tae mak' a wey
> For ane o' iron and steel,
> But though I'm auld I'm soople,
> An' my age I dinna feel.
> But yet if I'm no' wantit,
> I'll no tak' the huff.
> I'll jist resign an' mak' the wey
> For ane o' better stuff.[13]

Townhead Bridge, Kirkintilloch, before being replaced by a swing bridge in the 1930s.
East Dunbartonshire Libraries: The William Patrick Library, Kirkintilloch.

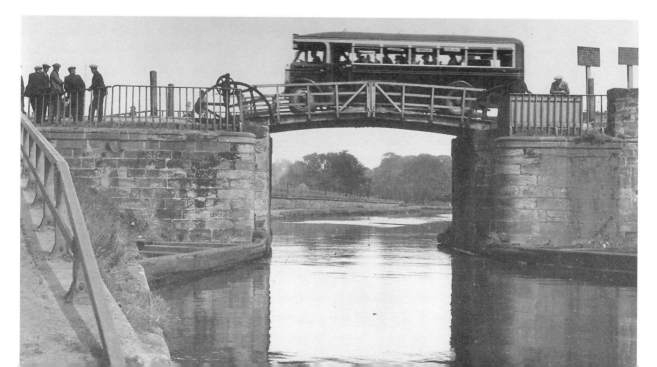

The opening of Ferry Road Bridge, Old Kilpatrick, 1934.

Lifting bridge at Temple nearing completion in the 1930s.

Calls to do away with the bridge grew and even the douce *Sunday Post* got in on the act in 1930 with an article about 'The Famous Bridge at Kirkintilloch'. The reporter elicited bad language from a bus driver, and marvelled at how he fitted his large vehicle over such a small structure. He made much of the signs restricting the weight of vehicles to three tons and their speed to two miles an hour—'As if that were possible!' A petition seeking the bridge's replacement started to circulate early in 1932. The town council needed little persuasion and after obtaining a 75 per cent Government grant commissioned Crouch & Hogg engineers to design a steel swing bridge. Contractors Sir William Arrol & Co. started work in early October and the poetic critic of 1921 was moved to sentimentality:

> Fareweel! Auld Brig, we'll think o' you,
> Yer fottygraf we'll keep in view.
> Tho' never steady ye were true
> Tae whatever cam';
> Wi' memories sweet we'll aft review
> Yer traffic jam!

The new bridge was opened on 2 June 1933 and *Gipsy Queen* sailed through to exercise the priority of canal traffic over road users.[14]

While the debate about Townhead Bridge had been going on, two massive lifting bridges, Cloberhill (1930) and Temple (1932), had been built. Both were part of larger road construction schemes. Cloberhill Bridge, on the extension to Glasgow's Great Western Road, was a new canal crossing, but Temple, on the Anniesland to Canniesburn Toll road, superseded the old bridge over Lock 27. It had been causing traffic bottlenecks and complaints for years. Other bridges followed: Dalgrain, 1933/34; Ferry Road, Old Kilpatrick, 1934; Lambhill, 1935; Bonnybridge and Hungryside, 1936; Auchinstarry, Kirkintilloch Hillhead and two bridges at Grangemouth, 1938. They were all built by Sir William Arrol & Co. and their construction was made possible by 75 per cent Ministry of Transport grants to replace weak bridges. Plans were also made to replace Twechar Bridge and the tram bridges at Camelon and Bainsford, but these were stopped by the Second World War.

Sir William Arrol & Co. also built a private swing bridge at Redding for Nobel's Explosive Works which had premises on both sides of the Union Canal. The Union's numerous road bridges and aqueducts did not initially impede the growth of road transport, but the restrictive size of these structures gradually began to tell. New bridges on the Falkirk to Maddiston Road at Polmont and the A8 at Broxburn bypassed existing crossings, but the canal was stopped in 1937 to replace Slateford Bridge with a splendid concrete aqueduct, allowing Slateford Road to be widened. There was never any prospect of reviving commercial traffic when the canal reopened.

Commercial traffic between the Union and Forth & Clyde Canals had ceased by 1933 and so the flight of locks from Bantaskine to Port Downie was abandoned and filled in. Cut short at both ends and little used, the Union Canal was now in danger of further damage, but suggestions that the city section should be drained were successfully opposed by Edinburgh's rowers. Writers paid nostalgic visits and pityingly described the 'decaying woodwork, neglected bridges, abandoned buildings, vacant windows, dignified isolation and festoons of weed'. The canal was clearly in a bad way and might have received some unwelcome attention if World War II had not taken people's minds off it.[15]

Construction of the Cloberhill lifting bridge, Great Western Road, Glasgow c.1930.

White Horse Distillers' puffer *Pibroch* passing through Cloberhill Bridge, Glasgow.

Slateford Bridge   Crown Copyright: Royal Commission on the Ancient and Historical Monuments of Scotland (Chrystal Collection).

blether at the bridge

Slateford Bridge is also known as Prince Charlie's Bridge. The Jacobite army set up camp nearby before entering Edinburgh in 1745—which would certainly have made an impact on the area—but it is hard to see how a canal structure can be associated with an event that took place over 70 years before it was built! Perhaps the name really belongs to the road bridge over the Water of Leith and popular myth has transferred it to the more impressive aqueduct over Slateford Road.

Slateford Bridge, built 1937 to replace the original in the upper picture.

Farm Bridge

East Dunbartonshire Libraries: The William Patrick Library, Kirkintilloch.

blether at the bridge

It carries a main road now, but originally the bridge at Bishopbriggs was an insubstantial private affair built on wooden piles. The landowner, Mr Stirling of Kenmure, had to be bought out so that a new bridge and cottage could be built. Local people used to call it Jellyhill Bridge and for over 100 years it was worked by the Brash family. Adam, the first 'Brash o' the Brig', started in 1838 and handed over to his son John after 57 years. He was there for 33 years before his son Davie took over, maintaining the family tradition into the 1940s.[5]

The Second World War

Weed and a derelict rowing stage at Bantaskine Bridge, Falkirk.

At the start of the war the Forth & Clyde Canal was seen as a useful defensive line. The Home Guard was detailed to open bridges and immobilise them, but training was patchy and the idea faintly silly because a determined mechanised army was unlikely to baulk at having to cross the canal. Stop-locks were built at Stockingfield, Firhill and Spiers Wharf, and a dam and weir was put in across the Cut of Junction at St Rollox to prevent flooding if the canal was bombed: and it was bombed, but not there.

Clydebank was hit on two successive nights in March 1941 in Scotland's worst air-raids. Houses and factories were wrecked and hundreds of lives lost. The wood yard at Singer's works was set alight by incendiary bombs on the first night and acted as a beacon for the second raid. Water mains were quickly destroyed, but the fire-fighters ran hoses to the canal which remained a useful source of water despite being damaged. That the canal survived at all was a matter of luck: one bomb narrowly missed the Dalmuir railway tunnel and another, which came down at Dalmuir Bridge, failed to explode. Less than a month later Clydeside was hit again and a bomb breached the canal at Lock 35, with the water flowing into Yoker Burn and causing a flood at Dumbarton Road.[16]

Maryhill was in the thick of it too. Seven people died when houses in Kilmun Street were wrecked by a land mine on the second night of the Clydebank raid. The target can only be guessed at, but the canal, railways, gasworks and MacLellan's Rubber Works could all have been on the hit list—if indeed the bomber pilots knew exactly where they were in the dark. A barrage balloon, manned by a Polish crew, was sited at Collina, beside Maryhill Locks. It was intended to deter low-level, accurate bombing, but may just have advertised a target area! Kelvin Dock boatyard was kept busy building landing craft for the D-day invasion and a roof was erected over the dry dock so that work could go on day and night. Each finished boat was sailed away by a naval petty officer and two ratings.

There may have been some aspiring naval recruits amongst the 1st West Lothian Sea Scouts when they mustered for the first time in May 1942 at Woodcockdale stables to the west of Linlithgow. The canal offered relatively safe water for them to learn boat-handling skills on, and the activity proved to be one of the most enduring on either canal. Their founder and first Scoutmaster, the Revd P.H.R. (Hugh) Mackay, went on to become a leading canal campaigner.[17]

blether at the bridge

Ruchill Bridge was known as Chapel, House Chapel, or Roughhill (Ruchill) Wester Bridge before acquiring its present name. Mrs G. Wardle took over as the canal's only female bridge keeper in 1925 when her husband, who had been bridge keeper since 1887, died. She retired in 1947.[6]

Ruchill Bridge

David Holgate

The empty and forlorn Manse Road Basin at Linlithgow.

Closure

Filling in the Grangemouth timber basins.

While the Scouts rowed on the Union and the Navy sailed its new craft out of the Forth & Clyde, a book called *Narrow Boat* was being written. Its author, Tom Rolt, described an epic journey on the decaying English canal system at the start of the war, and it so inspired a man named Robert Aikman that he sought a meeting with Rolt. The two agreed that the canals were in such a parlous state that a campaigning organisation was needed to save them, and in February 1946, at an inaugural meeting in London, the Inland Waterways Association (IWA) was formed. In the coming years it would have a significant influence on Government thinking.

Labour had won a landslide victory in the 1945 general election and embarked on an extensive programme of nationalisation. The railways and most of the canals came under state control on 1 January 1948. Canals were separated from railway management and placed under the Docks and Inland Waterways Executive of the giant British Transport Commission (BTC). Pre-war decline and neglect continued, and by the early 1950s the BTC was making ominous statements about the future of canals. The IWA took its campaign to Parliament and in 1953 managed to persuade MPs to set up an all-party committee on inland waterways.

The following year, the BTC set up a Board of Survey chaired by Lord Rusholme. It looked at canals purely in commercial terms, as transport providers, and placed them in three categories. First were those with development potential, the broad river navigations and canals that fed into docks; second was a group with sufficient value to make them worth keeping; and lastly were those waterways whose commercial prospects did not justify retention for navigation. Scotland's three lowland canals were in this group and faced a very real threat, but a cabinet reshuffle and a new Transport Minister brought a stay of execution. Another inquiry, with a broader remit than Lord Rusholme's, was set up in 1956 chaired by the managing director of the Pacific Steam Navigation Company, Leslie Bowes.[1]

Kilbowie Road Bridge

blether at the bridge

Singer's sewing machine factory beside Kilbowie Road Bridge contributed to the success of a colony of goldfish that thrived in the canal next to it. No one knows how the fish got there, but warm water, discharged into the canal from the works, created ideal conditions. Small boys used to go fishing for them and even managed to supplement their pocket money by selling little ones to pet shops.

Ayacucho, the boat of campaigner Douglas Russell, in Maryhill Locks.

Twechar Bridge under construction.
Crown Copyright: Royal Commission on the Ancient and Historical Monuments of Scotland (Sir William Arrol Collection).

The Bowes Report was published in July 1958. It broadly retained Lord Rusholme's three categories and was more positive about the English canals, but presented a bleak future for the Union and Monkland Canals, and the Forth & Clyde's Glasgow Branch. They were described as having 'no future potential as commercial navigations' and as a result their future lay in being redeveloped as roads, while maintaining their water supplies to industry. The report also recommended retaining the Forth & Clyde main line as a source of industrial water, but closing it to navigation. It recognised that this would be a severe blow to fishermen who used the canal regularly, but pointed out that the cost of keeping the canal open was a disguised subsidy to their industry. Savings to local authorities released from their obligations of manning and maintaining the opening bridges were trumpeted, and there was an ominous sting in the tail: a pointed reference highlighted the number of drowning accidents, particularly in the Monkland Canal. The endgame had begun.[2]

The issue of children drowning had grown since 1950 when residents of Linnvale raised a petition to close the canal.[3] Their action was taken up by Clydebank Town Council which tried to persuade others to press for closure. Kirkintilloch resisted, but Glasgow, while initially expressing concerns about water supplies to Pinkston Power Station, began to take an interest.[4] Newspapers initially took the view that it was the responsibility of parents and society to ensure child safety, but the press knows a bandwagon when it sees one and, for some papers, the tone changed. MPs, city councillors and the Glasgow Presbytery of the Church of Scotland all held meetings to highlight the problem. A Glasgow Canal Association was formed to campaign for safe canals—by which they meant filling them in or erecting fences. Despite giving dire warnings of the dangers, the association was appalled to discover that people were still playing football near the canals while others, including women with prams, were setting children a bad example by walking on the towpaths! Fences were erected, with predictable results—they were torn down and the warning notices thrown in the water.[5] The number of tragedies remained constant, at about two a year, but hostile meetings and a compliant press fanned the issue until it became inseparable from the debate about the future of the canals.[6]

The *West Lothian Courier* took a sudden interest in the Union Canal in the summer of 1949, reporting on its 'dreadful condition' and the death of a prize horse from drinking the water. The practice of young men swimming in water contaminated by dead dogs and leaks from an overhead sewage pipe raised fears of a typhoid epidemic, although claims that the canal had caused a scarlet fever outbreak in Winchburgh were dismissed.

The Edinburgh Development Plan of 1953 proposed making part of the Union Canal into a road, but industries, including the North British Rubber Co. which used 90,000 gallons of water an hour, opposed the idea. Industry's needs also prevented demolition of the aqueduct over the A9 at Linlithgow to allow the road to be widened, despite suggestions that the water flow could be maintained by a siphoning system. This industrial water-use was described as 'bunk' by an Edinburgh MP as he launched a campaign to do away with the 'foul smelling monstrosity' with its 'rats as big as kittens'. A committee was formed at a public meeting and it got up a petition of 3,000 signatures demanding that the canal should be drained, while declaring that it was 'not interested in what happens after that'.[7]

In 1956, with the canals receiving a stream of negative publicity, the

The *Ashton* returning to the Clyde past Netherton Farm.

George MacAngus.

***Opposite left:* Fishing boats at Temple Locks.**

The *Pearl o' Moray*, one of the little boats that had to leave the canal when it closed.

Bill Brodie.

BTC chose to encourage business. They took on more staff, installed new machinery, tackled arrears of maintenance and appointed a full-time manager.[8] In 1958 he announced plans for a cruising restaurant boat, but while that remained a dream he was able to welcome the first of six canal cars which two Glasgow taxi drivers intended to hire as pleasure boats between Lambhill and Kirkintilloch.[9] The following year two hire cruisers were put on the Union Canal at Drumshoreland, near Broxburn, but the tide of opinion was against these ideas. The Bowes Report had encouraged those who wanted rid of the canals to pursue closure. The advantages were talked up—Glasgow needed a road to run across the north of the city from Alexandra Parade to Great Western Road—and the disadvantages—that the city could not afford it—were ignored. Great concern was expressed in Fife about the devastating blow closure would mean for their fishing fleet. They got sympathy, but little else.[10]

Extraordinarily, with the canal's closure a hot topic, a new lifting bridge was installed at Twechar. It was opened in October 1960, but somebody, somewhere must have wished they had waited. The A80 Glasgow to Stirling road was about to be upgraded to dual-carriageway, with the Denny bypass section having to cross the canal at Castlecary. The canal's fate rested on the decision as to what form the crossing would take—an opening bridge costing £160,000 which would retain navigation, or a culvert which would close the canal.

The axe fell in June 1961 when, in a written answer to a question in the House of Commons, the Secretary of State for Scotland, John S. Maclay, announced the closure of the Forth & Clyde Canal to navigation but its retention as a channel for industrial water.[11] The authorities and individuals who had campaigned for closure welcomed the decision as 'inevitable', yet bizarrely hoped the canal would not become an eyesore or a danger.

'It will become both' warned the first letter of opposition to appear in the papers. It was written by a regular canal user and IWA member, Douglas Russell.[12] Supporting letters were written by other individuals and the IWA, which attacked the decision as 'an outrageous public scandal'. The association kept up a long-distance war of words, accusing the press of publishing 'hysterical bilge' and describing those who had welcomed closure as a 'gleeful cabal of canal wreckers' (which probably only stiffened their resolve to go ahead and wreck the canal). They also criticised the BTC for lacklustre management and for actually seeking closure of the canal. But the IWA's calls for a Scottish branch to fight the closure were not taken up, and with no local campaign to save it the canal was doomed. The Act to extinguish navigation rights was passed in March 1962, probably the first time that a working canal was closed by direct Government action!

Just before closure, in October 1962, the Glasgow University Railway Society chartered the little Clyde steamer *Ashton* and brought her into the canal. The intention was to sail to Kirkintilloch and then make a special run to Craigmarloch, but she fouled the propeller at Westerton and the delay waiting for divers meant cancellation of the Craigmarloch trip. She sailed back from Kirkintilloch to the Clyde the following day; the last passenger vessel to use the canal before closure.

A fishing boat was the last commercial vessel to go from coast to coast; a fitting end because fishermen had been amongst the first to use the canal. In 1794 the *Glasgow Advertiser* reported the passage of 50 boats going east after

Cutting down the lock gates was meant to make them safer, but these boys at Maryhill were unimpressed, and in much greater danger.

Sunk barge at Clydebank in the late 1960s.

the failure of the West Highland herring fishery, and since then inshore boats from both coasts had continued to use the canal to move between fishing grounds. Some sold their catch to canalside communities on the way through, others came into the canal specially to sell fish to local people, while lock keepers and wee boys who helped at the locks were given free fish. The fishermen who used the canal regularly were bitter about the way their views had been ignored. They would have been happy to see their fees more than double if it meant keeping the canal open, but no one talked to them about it, or the possibility of establishing fixed headroom bridges. And so the unusual closure of a fully operational canal was compounded by the sight of a working vessel passing from coast to coast on Boxing Day 1962.[13] A few days later, at midnight on 31 December, navigation was stopped and as the bells rang in a Happy New Year the canal died.

Death by 1,000 Culverts

Building the Armco culvert at Govan Cottage Bridge, Kelvindale, Glasgow.

The 'lone voices' who had spoken out against closure had been unable to stem the tide, but their predictions of what would happen were to prove unerringly accurate. Donald Bruce, writing in the *Scotsman* on 5 January 1963, thought that local politicians would be happy at the demise of what they called the 'Death Canal' but would be wrong to think that 'only a few fishermen and yachtsmen will suffer'. He predicted that 'the locks will be replaced by dams or pipes, and a few parts will be filled in and built on. The water level will be lowered by a foot or so to save bank maintenance. The staff who patrol and work on the canal will gradually be cut down. The bridge keepers will go. There will be no passing vessels. The reeds and waterweed will grow, and then indeed the lonely deserted banks will be a death trap for the children of the nearby towns'.

He was right. Drowning tragedies rose in the years following closure and calls for the canals to be filled in grew louder, but water supply and land drainage functions restricted the number of schemes that went ahead. The St Rollox Basin and part of the Monkland Canal were infilled in 1964 to make way for the Townhead interchange on the Glasgow motorway inner ring road and, two years later, in readiness for the next phase of motorway building, the basin between Ann Street Bridge and Colinton Street was filled in. The really big infillings of the 1960s, however, took place on the Monkland Canal in Coatbridge where schemes eliminated the canal from Sykeside to Blair Bridge. Government grants met 90 per cent of the cost, but at £750,000 infilling did not come cheap.[14]

The day-to-day management of the canals was now in the hands of a new authority, the British Waterways Board (BWB). It had been set up under the 1962 Transport Act which separated the British Transport Commission into three component parts: railways, docks and waterways. BWB came into being just as the Forth & Clyde was closed and for the rest of the 1960s presided over its descent into decay and dereliction. Lock gates were shorn of their balance beams and cut down to reduce water levels. Weirs were lowered, banks collapsed and rubbish accumulated in the increasingly weed-choked water. It was exactly as Donald Bruce had said it would be.

The A80 was quickly pushed across the canal at Castlecary on a drowned culvert. This consisted of two large-diameter pipes buried in solid infill below water level, with the road simply laid on top. Drowned culverts appear to have been a favourite with the planners and were used in 1964 to replace the tram

A tangle of neglect at Leamington Bridge.
Donald Mackinnon collection.

Port Dundas in decline.

Flotsam in Lock 27, Temple.

bridges at Camelon and Bainsford in Falkirk, and Dalmuir and Kilbowie Road at Clydebank.[15] Kirkintilloch's Townhead Bridge went the same way in 1967 and a similar culvert replaced Ruchill Bridge.

Two major sections to the west of Glasgow were infilled in the late 1960s: one between the Cloberhill Locks and Great Western Road, and the other for a new road, Duntreath Avenue. Armco culverts—corrugated metal tubes—were used for culverts at Govan Cottage Bridge and Bonnybridge, while some bascule bridges were replaced by fixed concrete decks and some of the swing bridges were simply fixed. The worst damage was reserved for Grangemouth where the expense of a culvert was avoided by using the old Carron Cut canal to take the water to the river. The main channel and the extensive timber basins were filled in—a cruel irony for the canal to be destroyed by the town it had created. (Although maybe Bo'ness enjoyed getting its own back—the infill material came from the Kinneil Colliery bing!) A road was laid along the route of the canal, and a warehouse was built across the sea lock and North Basin area. It was the only structure erected on the line of the canal during closure. Later, the M9 motorway was driven across the infilled canal at Dalgrain.

In Edinburgh the Union Canal had come to be regarded as the city's 'Sunset Boulevard', the fading star of a bygone era, and with the Forth & Clyde gone the eliminators turned their fire on it. The Bowes Report had noted that it supplied water to about fourteen industrial users, but dismissed its use by some pleasure craft as if they were of no consequence. By contrast, in 1960, West Lothian County Council Roads Committee agreed to prepare a scheme for the canal to be used by light craft, while at the same time seeking a solution to the problem of the narrow aqueduct on the A9 through Linlithgow.[16] But this was isolated foresight and by 1963 the Lochrin Basin boat-hire business was no longer operating, the building had become dilapidated and the boats lay around half sunk. Two children playing on them had to be rescued and a local councillor called a public protest meeting to highlight the dangers. Only the press turned up but he ploughed on, calling for the canal to be made safe— by turning it into a motorway! It did not become a road, but it was formally closed to navigation in August 1965 and quickly fell victim to the march of 'progress'.[17]

Construction of the Wester Hailes housing estate, on the western outskirts of Edinburgh, began in November 1967 and over a mile of the canal was culverted to make way for it.[18] The canal also disappeared into a drowned culvert when the Dechmont to Newhouse section of the M8 motorway was constructed between December 1968 and November 1970. These culverts were arguably worse than anything on the Forth & Clyde; Wester Hailes because its size and location made restoration immensely difficult, and the M8 because it also severed the towpath, the only place where the cross-country path was cut.[19]

It could have been worse. In the late 1960s Stirling County Council put forward a plan to fill in five miles of the canal from Glen Village to Muiravonside with the material from pit bings. They also hoped to improve roads and make pedestrian use of the bridge at Polmont safer, but they faced resolute opposition. A well-attended conference at Edinburgh University in December 1969 brought together concerned individuals and groups including the Scottish Wildlife Trust, the Scottish Society for Industrial Archaeology, academics from Strathclyde University and Tam Dalyell MP. With his help the issue was forced to a public inquiry which concluded in November 1970 after two postponements. The

Kelvin Dock in a state of dereliction.

Sheet piling at Lock 36: one end of a culvert made to
build Duntreath Avenue.

The culverted A80 at Castlecary.

Lock 32 cut down and culverted to accommodate the lowering of Blairdardie Road.

David Holgate.

reporter recommended rejection of the council's plan and, after some delay, the Secretary of State for Scotland agreed. It was a stunning victory; the canal had been saved on environmental, heritage and amenity grounds only a few years after it had been closed![20]

It was also only two years after the Transport Act of 1968 had confirmed the pariah status of Scotland's lowland canals. The Act used the three categories first proposed by Lord Rusholme's Board of Survey in 1955 to create two main groups, 'commercial' and 'cruising' waterways, while giving BWB the job of maintaining 'the remainder' in a safe condition at minimal cost. It was a recipe for continuing decline. Respective chairmen of the Board came to Scotland in the early 1970s to discuss the future with interested parties, but there was no money and no prospect of reopening what were now referred to as remainder canals.

Drowned culverts were put in on the A801 Lathallan to Bowhouse road east of Polmont; at Preston Road, Linlithgow; Greendykes Road, Broxburn and Kingsknowe Road, Edinburgh. An Armco culvert replaced Muiravonside Bridge on the Maddiston to Whitecross road. Barriers were erected to prevent pedestrian use of the great aqueducts for safety reasons, and in Edinburgh the path between Yeaman Place and Gilmore Park was blocked by the rubber works for security.

Remarkably, amidst the gloom, Glasgow provided a silver lining. The city had been planning what was called the Maryhill Motorway for some years and had even looked at the possibility, in advance of presenting detailed plans, of obtaining a 75 per cent Government grant to pipe and fill the Glasgow Branch from Port Dundas to Stockingfield. Spurs from the main M8 ring-road had been constructed with the expectation of continuing the road along the route of the canal, but Maryhill folk took exception to the plans when they were made public in 1972. The road would run through heavily populated areas, past Charles Rennie Mackintosh's Queen's Cross Church, jeopardising his Ruchill Street Church Hall, and threatening the East Park Home for mentally handicapped children with demolition. It would get commuters from Milngavie into the city faster, but would wreck Maryhill (the uncertainty had already blighted the area), and the strength of local opposition killed the plan.[21] People-power in another part of Glasgow also beat plans for the Crow Road Expressway. It was another road designed to ease commuter journeys from outside the city and would have wiped out the Temple Locks area if it had gone ahead.

Glasgow Corporation also commissioned two studies from landscape consultants in the early 1970s which were carried out against the background of the motorway proposals. The second, completed in 1974, offered an upgrading of the mess that closure had left, but few people were attracted to the proposals when they were exhibited. Even the consultants seemed unconvinced, stating 'that those canals . . . rendered un-navigable are less functional, less visually attractive and less acceptable as a feature . . . than those where water based activity has been encouraged'.

The 1968 Transport Act had also established a Government advisory body, the Inland Waterways Amenity Advisory Council (IWAAC). Its members inspected the canals in 1974 and were appalled at the damage. Their report to the Secretary of State for the Environment recommended a detailed study to assess the canals' potential and stated that 'Nothing further should be done'. But it was: even while IWAAC was making its inspection other schemes were

The west end of the Wester Hailes culvert.

The culverted M8 motorway near Broxburn.

Drowned culvert at Greendykes Road, Broxburn.

in the pipeline. In 1975 Glasgow Road Bridge near Kirkintilloch on the Forth & Clyde Canal was replaced by an Armco culvert, despite a major campaign supported by the local MP, Margaret Bain. There was vociferous opposition too to proposals to shallow the canal through Clydebank, but that scheme went ahead in 1978. A new road, Argyll Road, was also built over a box culvert at Whitecrook. The last culvert was constructed in 1980 at Abbots Road, Falkirk, but by then attitudes were changing and the local authorities agreed to raise the road to an appropriate height if the canal was ever brought back into use.

The infillings, road schemes and hostile opposition had finally run out of steam. Millions of pounds had been spent on achieving a mess of overgrown, rubbish-strewn dereliction. The canals had been wrecked, but in the process they had found some friends.

A truck passes through a canal bridge in Glasgow's east end during construction of the M8 motorway along the route of the Monkland Canal from Blackhill to West Maryston (Easterhouse) in the early 1970s.[22]

Barrier on Slateford Aqueduct towpath, erected for safety reasons.
Donald Mackinnon collection.

The last culvert—at Abbots Road, Falkirk— with a boat crossing Scotland the hard way!

Revival

Launch of the *Lady Margaret* restaurant boat in 1987.

A number of individuals had watched the canals' closure and culverting with dismay, but the defeat of Stirlingshire's infilling proposals encouraged them to fight on. In May 1971 a meeting was held at Edinburgh University to set up a Scottish Inland Waterways Association (SIWA). Its first chairman was that redoubtable campaigner of ten years earlier, Douglas Russell. SIWA saw itself as a sister organisation to the IWA which had tried to save Scotland's canals from its base south of the border. Now there was a Scottish IWA and the fight-back had begun. There was a public opinion mountain to climb. The closure of the canals was still fresh in people's minds and the new organisation knew that attitudes had to change before any real progress could be made. It dug in for the long haul.

Independently, Glasgow students held a huge clean-up of the Maryhill/ Temple area as part of their annual charities appeal in November 1971. With help from the city's cleansing department they removed 1,000 tons of rubbish, discovered a stolen car and got a lot of publicity.[1] The core of these young volunteers went on to form the nucleus of a squad of SIWA 'navvies', organising work-parties across the country. They were even complimented on the floor of the House of Commons on 1 July 1976 when Jim Craigen, MP for Maryhill, raised the state of the Forth & Clyde Canal in an adjournment debate.

From the start, Linlithgow was a centre of activity. The local Civic Trust along with the West Lothian History and Amenity Society organised clean-ups and other activities on the canal. Divers from HMS *Lochinvar* and Linlithgow fire brigade helped to raise a sunk barge, U66, in March 1972, and the canal's 150th anniversary was marked by SIWA's first rally, held at Linlithgow on 30 September 1972.[2] Twelve canoes, three dinghies and ten powered craft sailed out to Philpstoun and back in glorious autumn sunshine.[3] The plan then was to open up the eight and a half miles of canal between Linlithgow and Broxburn. The British Waterways Board agreed to help with channel clearance, and the

Volunteers working to clean up the Maryhill Locks and Basins, 1975.

The first SIWA rally at Linlithgow with the salvaged scow U66 in the foreground.

Linlithgow Union Canal Society.

Competitors in the Drambuie marathon portaging at Underwood Lockhouse.

Weaving through the weed on the Drambuie marathon.

Volunteers in the process of removing 300 tons of rubbish from Lochrin Basin in 1977 as part of a weekend of action promoted by Granada Television.

Donald Mackinnon collection.

possibility of having the stretch navigable the following year was confidently predicted, but the scheme faded as a battle of ideas developed.

Some enthusiasts wanted more immediate progress on their own bit of canal and began to set up local groups. The Strathkelvin Canal Park Association (SCAPA) was formed in the Kilsyth/Cumbernauld area in 1973. It created slipway and jetty facilities for small boats at Auchinstarry and Wyndford. At much the same time, the Calders Canal Association tried to establish a marina at Calders Crescent, Wester Hailes, but vandals wrecked the unfinished building.[4]

SIWA was worried that these groups would dilute its effectiveness as a national body, and when the Linlithgow Union Canal Society (LUCS) was formed in 1975 it had to rethink its overall strategy. The association had looked on the town as a centre from which improvements elsewhere would flow, but although LUCS was essentially a local group its impact was felt over a wider area. To begin with the new society used U66, renamed *Queen of the Union*, for horse-drawn boat trips, but found it unsuitable for public cruising and sent it to the Scottish Maritime Museum at Irvine for them to restore and exhibit. LUCS opened their own museum at Manse Road Basin in 1977 and, the following year, launched the delightful little trip boat *Victoria*. The drowned culvert at Preston Road prevented her going west to the Avon Aqueduct, but she became an instant hit sailing out towards Philpstoun and back, weed permitting! The towpath through the town was also improved by the society with help from boys from the Polmont borstal. LUCS originally shared the stables at the basin with a canoe club, but by 1990 had taken over the whole building and renovated it as a tearoom. They added a new vessel, *St Magdalene*, to their 'fleet' in 1995.[5]

LUCS also took over the running of the Drambuie Cross-Scotland Canal Marathon in 1978. This glorious event had started in 1973 with sponsorship from the *Daily Express*. Crews of two had to navigate an inflatable boat, at a set speed, powered by an outboard engine, from Edinburgh to Kelvingrove Park in Glasgow. The River Kelvin proved to be a boat ripper, although SIWA neatly blamed the state of the canals for all the damage! Subsequent events were confined to the canals and, with a couple of exceptions, went from Glasgow to Edinburgh. These marathons were enormous fun for all concerned, but they also showed people from one side of the country to the other that the canals came from somewhere and went somewhere, and were not just local duck ponds.

At Ratho the canal had started to come alive again thanks to the efforts of one man, Ronnie Rusack. He took over the run-down Bridge Inn, improved it and in 1974 added to its amenity by launching a purpose-built restaurant boat, *Pride of the Union*. It was the 250th anniversary of the publication of a volume by Joseph Mitchell, the 'poet of Ratho', in which he set out his vision of the area's resurgence from its then desolate state. It contained two remarkably prophetic lines:

> Bridges and boats for pleasure crowd the scene,
> And ne'er was Ratho known so sweet and clean.

The prophesy had a few years to run before it really came true. Initially the boat struggled on the silted-up, weed-choked, rubbish-strewn channel, but after a big effort the water was cleared. The '*Pride*' was joined in 1987 by another restaurant boat, *Countess of Edinburgh*, which was later renamed *Pride of Belhaven*, and by a day boat, *Ratho Princess*. Boats for pleasure were indeed beginning to crowd the scene. The Bridge Inn was extended over the years and

Vaulting the canal at Ratho—one of many crowd-pulling events staged by the Edinburgh Canal Centre.

Cambridge University students punt to victory in a one-sided race against the Honourable Society of Edinburgh Boaters, who made failure and falling in into an art form.

Below left: Seagull Trust boathouse at Bantaskine, Falkirk.

Hugh McGinley.

New aqueduct over the Edinburgh bypass road.

the whole complex was additionally named the Edinburgh Canal Centre.

Ratho also became the base for the Seagull Trust's first boat *St John Crusader* in 1979. The trust's aim was to provide free cruising for disabled people and it was set up through the dogged determination of SIWA's vice chairman, the Revd Hugh Mackay. The *Mackay Seagull*, launched in 1986, was named after him. Further boating operations were established at Kirkintilloch and Falkirk in 1984, with boats built by shipyard apprentices and named after their yards. The Falkirk boat, *Govan Seagull*, started its operations on the Forth & Clyde Canal at Lock 16 because of water problems on the Union, but was later moved up to operate out of Port Maxwell until a splendid boathouse was built for it at Bantaskine in the early 1990s. A less splendid one was erected at Kirkintilloch for *Yarrow Seagull*, its fortress-like appearance a legacy of SIWA's constant battle with vandalism in the 1970s.

While all this activity was developing, the local and statutory authorities struggled with the dilemma of derelict canals and insufficient finance to do anything with them. Falkirk Town Council bucked the trend in 1973. With the aid of Government environmental grants they landscaped the banks of both canals in the town, making them appear much better than elsewhere. Other sections of towpath on both canals were improved by job creation schemes.[6]

A joint working party of local and national authorities responsible for the Union Canal was set up in 1971 and two years later its report recommended developing the canal for recreational use. As a result a Union Canal Development Group was formed in January 1975 comprising the British Waterways Board, Countryside Commission, Scottish Development Department and local authorities. The group's findings, presented in 1976, led to the setting up of a Union Canal Project jointly sponsored by Lothian and Central Regional Councils and the Countryside Commission. It was intended to run for only two years, but in that time was expected to stimulate interest and generate a range of activities. It was a huge task, but project officer Jane Clark, who was appointed in January 1979, tackled it enthusiastically. She produced a range of leaflets, publicity material and audio-visual aids, and also encouraged the development of local canal societies in the hope that they would carry on promoting the canal when her job ceased. Some groups predated the project and most flowered only briefly, but by 1981 societies had been set up at Broxburn, Winchburgh, Wester Hailes and Kingsknowe, Ratho and Falkirk.

All this activity on the Union Canal was to help in one major way. In the late 1970s Lothian Regional Council's highways department published plans for Edinburgh's outer city bypass road, which proposed severing the canal just north of Calder Road. There was a logic to it: the proposed culvert would be only a few hundred yards west of the infilled section at Wester Hailes. SIWA objected, arguing that the development group report had already suggested a way of reinstating the canal through Wester Hailes, and that nothing should be done which would prevent navigation being re-established in the future. BWB weighed in against the plans too and, after a vigorous campaign, the council agreed to put the road in cutting and build a new aqueduct. It was a major victory, because if the canal had been blocked restoration into Edinburgh would have been made immeasurably harder and perhaps impossible. The aqueduct was opened in May 1987.

Ten years earlier Bonnington Aqueduct, to the west of Ratho, had been widened for road improvements with a steel trough replacing the stone original

An old maintenance barge refloated by volunteers and pressed into service as a trip boat at Maryhill, 1975.

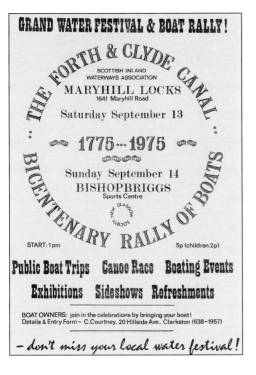

GRAND WATER FESTIVAL & BOAT RALLY!

THE FORTH & CLYDE CANAL

SCOTTISH INLAND WATERWAYS ASSOCIATION

MARYHILL LOCKS
1641 Maryhill Road

Saturday September 13

1775···1975

Sunday September 14
BISHOPBRIGGS
Sports Centre

BICENTENARY RALLY OF BOATS

START: 1 pm   5p (children 2p)

Public Boat Trips   Canoe Race   Boating Events
Exhibitions   Sideshows   Refreshments

BOAT OWNERS: join in the celebrations by bringing your boat!
Details & Entry Form – C.Courtney, 20 Hillside Ave., Clarkston (638-1957)

– don't miss your local water festival!

Left: **A wet day at Kirkintilloch: day one of Clyde '76, a three day rolling rally.**

Forth & Clyde Canal Society.

Rudder of a scow found during the dredging of Maryhill basins in 1985.

to keep the navigation intact (if a foot shallower than the original). In the late 1970s the Avon, Almond and Slateford Aqueducts had also been renovated, with the original iron troughs rebolted, new wooden fenders fitted and railings repaired. The towpaths were also reopened.

While the Union Canal's resurgence progressed steadily through the 1970s, the grim fight for the Forth & Clyde continued under the SIWA banner. Work parties to clean up the canal were organised at Old Kilpatrick, Dalmuir and all points east to Kirkintilloch. Sunk barges were raised and pressed into service as trip boats. Rallies, preceded by major clean-ups, were held at Ruchill and Maryhill in 1973 and 1974, and over two days at Maryhill and Bishopbriggs in 1975. In 1976 a three-day rolling rally, sponsored by Radio Clyde, started on a wet Saturday at Kirkintilloch, moved to Bishopbriggs on a sunny Sunday and on to Maryhill on the Monday. In those days the boats had to be beached, for security, on the old slipway at Kirkintilloch, but getting them back from Maryhill after three hard days went horribly wrong in the wee small hours of the Tuesday morning when a Land Rover and pick-up truck sank to their axles in mud! Even the Land Rover had to be towed out, but the fight went on and the campaigning of these die-hards reaped its reward.

In 1977 the local authorities along the Forth & Clyde Canal set up a working party which agreed to prepare a Local (Subject) Plan; a set of planning guidelines for the canal. Politically-aware enthusiasts realised the significance of this and pushed for the formation of a Forth & Clyde Canal Society (FCCS) to match the plan area. It was set up in 1980 and SIWA's battle-hardened campaigners in the west were drawn into it, along with SCAPA members. Shorn of its principal activists, SIWA adopted an umbrella role, but the campaign it had started ten years earlier was now being taken forward by FCCS. The political focus had shifted to the west.

The society developed boating activities to support political campaigning and pulled off a public relations masterstroke by purchasing, for £5 each, two old Clyde passenger ferries; boats much loved in Glasgow folk memory. They were in bad condition, so one was disposed of, but the other was restored, renamed *Ferry Queen* and put on the canal in 1982 at Glasgow Road Bridge. She was moved—with some difficulty—into Glasgow in the late 1980s and early 1990s to take the campaign to a new area. FCCS also raised the money to build a new boat, *Gipsy Princess*. She was delivered in 1990 and based at Auchinstarry to give substance to the society's attempts to influence the proposed upgrading of the A80 from Stepps to Haggs to motorway standard. The choice was stark; either a new road through the environmentally-sensitive Kelvin Valley which could have ruined the canal, or an upgrade of the existing road that offered the chance of restored navigation at Castlecary. Strong passions were stirred on both sides of a debate that went on for over a decade.

The Forth & Clyde Canal Society became something of a misnomer after only a few months because in June 1980, after meetings held by the local authorities for the Falkirk area, the Falkirk and District Canals Society (FDCS) was formed. FCCS and FDCS worked closely together and organised large rally events in 1985 and 1990. The latter, a trail-boat rally at the former Scottish Tar Distillers site at Falkirk, was promoted under a joint SIWA/IWA banner and attracted boats from across the two canals and south of the border.

The political initiative that led to FCCS's formation, the Forth & Clyde Canal Local (Subject) Plan, was arguably the single most important development

Ferry Queen.

Ruchill Bridge being rebuilt as part of the Glasgow Canal Project. In the foreground are the remains of the drowned culverts.

St Magdalene at the rebuilt Preston Road Bridge, Linlithgow.

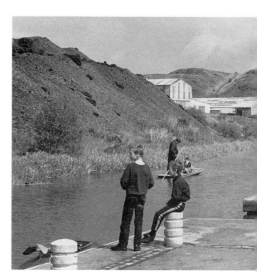

This refloated maintenance barge was used in the mid-1980s as a work boat for the Denny-Bonnybridge Project, a three-year scheme designed to carry out a range of improvements in the area.

New jetty and slipway at Stewartfield, Broxburn.

Linlithgow Union Canal Society.

on either canal during the years of closure. Although the process of preparing the plan was led by Strathclyde Regional Council and Falkirk District Council, all the local authorities on the canal backed it. The plan was progressed and monitored by committees with representation from the local authorities, BWB, the Countryside Commission and FCCS and FDCS on behalf of the voluntary sector. A public inquiry was held before it was adopted in 1987, but the impact was felt before that. A huge clean-up of the Maryhill Locks area, led by Strathclyde Region, took place in 1985. New bridges were built to the plan's proposed headroom standard of ten feet at Temple in 1984, Craigmarloch in 1985 and Kirkintilloch in 1990. Other works like towpath upgrading, environmental improvements and lock re-gating were also carried out under the local plan.

In 1986, with the political climate changing, BWB announced the £2.6 million Glasgow Canal Project, an ambitious plan to reopen twelve miles of canal from Temple to Kirkintilloch. It involved reinstating Maryhill Locks and restoring Ruchill, Firhill, Govan Cottage, Farm and Glasgow Road Bridges. A funding partnership of Government agencies, local authorities and European sources was assembled, but the money did not match ambitions and by the time the project was ceremonially launched at Maryhill Locks in March 1988 Govan Cottage and Farm Bridges had been omitted. Firhill Bridge, renamed Nolly Brig for publicity purposes, was reopened in 1990; Ruchill and Glasgow Road Bridges followed soon after.

In 1987/88 the old Scottish Tar Distillers site at Falkirk was cleaned up in a scheme funded by BWB, the Scottish Development Agency and Central Regional Council. Tar, which had caused massive pollution to the Forth & Clyde Canal was removed from the channel. It had flowed into the water from ruptured tanks during the fire of 1973 that led to the plant's closure.

In 1990 the local authorities in the Glasgow area set up the Forth & Clyde Canal Community Project to promote the safe use of the canal in the city. It ran events aimed at encouraging young people to take part in activities like canoeing or wildlife study. Another project, a community boat called the *Nolly Barge,* was set up as a publicly-funded charitable organisation to provide a different kind of experience, mainly for young people from deprived areas. She had twelve bunks and was designed to sit low in the water, to fit under Farm Bridge after the Glasgow Canal Project had failed to raise it!

Two other schemes were implemented using the same funding model as the Glasgow Canal Project. The £1.75 million West Lothian Canal Project restored navigation on the Union Canal to the west of Linlithgow by replacing the drowned culvert at Preston Road with a bridge and repairing the embankment at Kettlestoun. It had been badly breached in the early 1980s. The £360,000 Clydebank Canal Project reinstated bascule bridges at Dalmuir Farm, Ferrydyke and Bowling, and regated Lock 37 at Old Kilpatrick. The towpath was also resurfaced.

A number of commercial developments also built on the canals' more positive image. New pub/restaurants were set up at Glasgow Road Bridge, Temple, Underwood and Camelon Bridge. Old pubs like the Union Inn and the Canal Inn at Camelon were given a new lease of life, although sadly the rough and ready Red Lion at Bainsford became an antique shop. A fish and chip boat was put on the shallowed canal bottom at Clydebank. Housing developments went up at Maryhill and Temple, and there were similar

The canal coming alive again—filming for a BBC drama serial at Lock 16 in 1987.

Ferry Queen at Maryhill, 1990.

developments beside the Union Canal at Merchiston Village in Edinburgh and the old St Magdalene Distillery in Linlithgow. The former City of Glasgow Grain Mills, Port Dundas Sugar Refinery and Canal Company offices at Spiers Wharf were restored as part of a splendid housing and commercial development. Two restaurant boats, the *Caledonian* and the *Lady Margaret*—'the cruising canalboat with the gourmet galley'—were also established at Glasgow Road Bridge in the 1980s.

BWB began to develop community links in 1984 by appointing a leisure officer and also a dedicated ranger for the Union Canal and a project officer for the Forth & Clyde. The Board also held a public meeting in 1986 which led to the establishment of the Edinburgh Canal Society. By the end of the decade the new society had established a collection of small boats and a base for them opposite Harrison Park. Their proudest achievement was the restoration of the historic launch *Kelvin* with a grant from the National Lottery Heritage Fund. A new society was also set up in the Broxburn area in the 1990s.

The Union Canal did not have a local plan, but some developments took place nonetheless. In 1982 the Scottish Development Agency funded a jetty and slipway facility at Stewartfield, on the west side of Greendykes Road at Broxburn. The canal was dredged from Port Maxwell through the tunnel in 1987 and on to Redding the following year. The tunnel was closed while safety checks were made, but reopened in 1988 allowing the Seagull Trust to operate through it. The trust was also the principal beneficiary of Hermiston Quay, a jetty facility built in 1994/95 beside Gogar Station Road. It was funded by Lothian and Edinburgh Enterprise Ltd. and built in association with the Edinburgh Green Belt Trust by British Waterways (BW); the word 'Board' had been dropped in 1988.

Under Strathclyde Regional Council's positive leadership the Forth & Clyde Canal Local Plan had made a huge impact, but with even more improvements in the pipeline, local government was reorganised. New unitary authorities replaced regional and district councils. Glasgow City Council took over the running of the committees, but for a while the plan marked time as the new councils reordered their financial priorities. Many local authority representatives on the committees were changed, while British Waterways and the canal societies provided the continuity. It was a crucial time; British Waterways had just announced the Millennium Link project.

Ratho Princess, a delightful passenger cruiser dating from the 1930s, was brought to Scotland in 1991 as the *Princess Victoria* and sailed for a few seasons at Kirkintilloch before being taken to Ratho where she was carefully restored.

Cyclists on the upgraded towpath near Lambhill.

The restored Spiers Wharf, Port Dundas.

Linlithgow Union Canal Society's trip boat *Victoria*. Although resembling a Victorian steam packet boat she was actually built as a diesel powered vessel in 1974.

Pride of the Union at the Edinburgh Canal Centre in 1997.

Govan Seagull heads west from the Falkirk tunnel.

Gipsy Princess near Auchinstarry on a busy day!

Launching the Millennium Link at Ratho, October 1994.

Enthusiasts celebrate the award of the Millennium Commission grant on St Valentine's Day, 1997!

JANET TELFOR

The Millennium Link

The Falkirk Wheel nearing completion, December 2001.

British Waterway's Director, Scotland, Jim Stirling (left), the driving force behind the project, with Millennium Commissioner, the Earl of Dalkeith.

British Waterways went public in October 1994 with a plan to seek funding from the newly established National Lottery to restore the canals and use them as a catalyst for the regeneration of the areas through which they passed. Many places along the route had been left blighted by the demise of old industries and it was a bold vision to see that they could be revitalised with reopened canals.

The bid was aimed at the Millennium Commission, the funding body set up to mark the coming millennium with a number of landmark projects. To fit this criterion, the project's proposed centrepiece was a huge rotating boat-lift, designed to link the two canals together again at Falkirk. Nothing like it had been built in the world before, and the hope was that the commission would see it as a millennial structure for central Scotland. The project name, the Millennium Link, therefore alluded to the hoped-for source of funding and the boat-lift which would provide the missing link between the canals. Other links would also be re-established from sea to sea and city to city.

The bid was sent to the commission in April 1995 and if optimism won financial backing the cheque would have been in the return post. It was not. The project was put on a 'B list' and for the next two years British Waterways was engaged in an almost constant process of revising, recosting, rebidding and answering a plethora of detailed questions.

The commission needed to be convinced about many things, one of which was the level of public support. To test it, a petition was got up in the autumn of 1995. The first signatures were gathered by the Forth & Clyde Canal Society on a bus tour to the Crinan Canal, but from that small beginning the petition gathered momentum. It was circulated widely where people who had an interest would see it, and canal societies took it to shopping centres close to the two canals. People took time to share their views on the likelihood of lottery cash being spent in their areas, and although many were sceptical, they signed

Pouring concrete at Govan Cottage Bridge, September 1999.

Erecting a new footbridge on the line of the old Blairdardie Road, January 2000.

Casting bridge pilasters at Lock 16, Camelon, April 2000.

and in the course of six weeks over 30,000 signatures were gathered. It was a remarkable effort and it answered a crucial question, but British Waterways had to grapple with many more!

Two of the 1960s infilling schemes, Wester Hailes and Grangemouth, presented major challenges. British Waterways realised from the outset that Wester Hailes was vital to the project's success and that if it proved impossible to reinstate the canal there, the prospect of overall success would be low. They discussed plans at length with local groups and tried to answer concerns regarding safety and prospects for employment. When the Millennium Commissioners came to investigate the project, they met with community representatives and were impressed by what they heard. Hopes were raised, but the positive impression gained at Wester Hailes was countered by concerns over reconnecting the cut-off eastern end of the Forth & Clyde to the River Carron. A new canal through Grangemouth Docks was the preferred option, but this would require extra funding and there were practical difficulties concerning its siting. The other possibility was a realigned Carron Cut making a direct connection to the river where tides and low bridges would restrict the navigation. Eventually money, or the lack of it, resolved the dilemma in favour of the direct route.

Just before Christmas 1996, as yet another deadline passed, concern grew that the project had been sidelined, but early the following year events moved quickly. The Government announced their decision (later put on hold by the incoming Labour administration) to upgrade the existing A80 to motorway standard, thus saving the Kelvin Valley and resolving outstanding issues as to

Rebuilding Lock 32 at Cloberhill, May 2000.

Stone masons repairing Lock 31 at Cloberhill, January 2000.

Dredging the Union Canal at Drumshoreland, near Broxburn, October 1998.

Assembling the new lifting bridge at Twechar, September 2000.

The canal below Lock 4 at Abbots Road being reinstated by Falkirk Council, March 2001.

what bridges a restored canal would need. A couple of weeks later, on St Valentine's Day 1997, the commission announced its intention to award the project £32.4 million.

There was celebrating, but it was tinged with the realisation that the estimated cost of the full project was £78.4 million and another hurdle still had to be jumped. Large lottery awards had to be matched by other funds, and for the rest of that year British Waterways worked to confirm the commitment of the project's partners—the European Regional Development Fund (ERDF), Scottish Enterprise and its local enterprise companies, local authorities and indeed themselves. This matching funding was almost all in place by late 1997 when the bomb dropped. A decision on ERDF funds made only about half of what was expected available. The project faced a serious shortfall and possible collapse.

Some time before, the Forth & Clyde Canal Local Plan committees had been re-formed as the Lowland Canals Steering Committee and its Advisory Group by adding West Lothian and City of Edinburgh Councils. A packed meeting, with members of both committees present, was held to discuss the funding crisis. The atmosphere was electric and the ERDF funders were left in no doubt as to the strength of support for the project. Further meetings and high-level lobbying kept the issue on the boil until April 1998 when the Secretary of State for Scotland, Donald Dewar, announced that funding guarantees were in place. The project was going ahead!

Camelon Bridge

blether at the bridge

There have been five different crossings at Camelon. First the road went under the canal through an aqueduct, exposed in the side of the excavation (circled), but because the art of building on the skew had not been developed the canal took a shallow S-bend to accommodate it. A bascule bridge was next, followed by a tram swing bridge and, when the canal was closed, a drowned culvert. A new bridge was built for the Millennium Link, but there is still a kink in the canal here.

Pouring concrete at Greendykes Road, Broxburn, August 1999.

Remaking the canal at Wester Hailes, April 2001.

It took almost a year for British Waterways to refine their plans, obtain planning permission and seek tenders for the first contracts, but on 12 March 1999 a ceremony was held to celebrate the start of the work. It took place on the side of Lock 31 in Donald Dewar's Glasgow Anniesland parliamentary constituency when, watched by invited guests and bemused local residents, he dug the first spadeful of earth. Before all the guests had left, the contractors began clearing the area to start work.

At the same time work began on four Union Canal bridges and, bit by bit over the next two years, the two canals were turned into a series of construction sites across the country. Culverts were removed and nearly 30 bridges built—including a unique drop-lock under the new bridge at Dalmuir. New opening bridges were made and old ones reinstated. Aqueducts, weirs and masonry bridges were refurbished. New locks were built, old ones made good and new sets of gates were installed. Over three miles of new canal were created, 300,000 tons of silt were dredged from the old and 51 miles of towing path were upgraded and resurfaced.

While all this was going on the rotating boat-lift at Falkirk, which had been a key element in persuading funders to back the project, also began to take shape. The process started on the drawing board (if architects and engineers use drawing boards in this computer age!) where the design went through a number of changes before emerging as a spectacular, twenty-first century iconic structure. There was nothing like it anywhere else in the world. It would be a unique attraction for Scotland, and in the country's grand tradition of using

Infill material heaped up to make a road down the middle of the canal at Clydebank for dump trucks to remove dredged infill without spoiling the canal banks, October 1999.

Four phases of the Dalmuir drop-lock:

April 2000

August 2000

October 2000

May 2001

Boats from Ratho and Linlithgow meet for the first time during celebrations to mark the reopening of the Union Canal under the M8, May 2000.

Constructing the aqueduct piers for the Falkirk Wheel, April 2001.

the most prosaic and obvious names for such things (like the Forth Bridge) it would be called the 'Falkirk Wheel'. It was to be built on the former Scottish Tar Distillers site, where the volunteers had invited the world to their trail-boat rally in 1990.

To get to the wheel the Union Canal was to be extended from a point close to Port Maxwell. The new section of canal would cross Greenbank Road on a new aqueduct and from there run along beside the railway for about a mile. It would then drop through two locks, turn 90°, go through a new tunnel under the railway and the Roman Antonine Wall, and emerge on the aqueduct leading to the wheel itself. At its base would be a large circular basin with a visitor centre alongside. A lock would give boats access to and from the Forth & Clyde Canal and a swing bridge would do the same for towpath users. It would be a canal system in microcosm with the potential to become a major new tourist attraction.

The project received some unwelcome attention in early October 1999 when the side of an excavation for a new lock at Bainsford collapsed. It was uncomfortably close to some housing and so the lock-site was moved, but work continued there and elsewhere until May 2000 when two sections of canal were ready for reopening. The first was at Broxburn on the Union Canal, when, with great ceremony, the M8 and Greendykes Road Bridges were inaugurated. Muiravonside and Lathallan Road Bridges were also completed at the same time. Two weeks later, Kirkintilloch's Townhead Bridge and Farm Bridge at Bishopbriggs were ceremonially reopened.

A bus party of tourists inspects Muiravonside Bridge, May 2000.

Millie the fabulous fish comes up through Lock 16 to start the celebrations to mark the reopening of the Forth & Clyde Canal, May 2001.

Millie the broken-down fish being towed past bemused swans at Twechar.

The little hamlet of Tintock, east of Kirkintilloch, welcomes the boats' return.

The canal bites back at the A80.

Navigation was restored to the whole of the Forth & Clyde Canal on the last weekend of May 2001. Boats came through from the west and up from the Forth to Lock 16 where huge crowds gathered to watch the ceremony. A giant floating fish called Millie (short for Millennium) cut the tape and set off for the west followed by the flotilla of boats. Alas Millie's machinery did not match her splendid appearance and broke down after a few hundred yards. Throughout the weekend crowds turned out to see the fabulous fish and although it spent much of the time under tow their enthusiasm was undimmed. Some keeled boats had problems with the depth of the channel and the drop-lock at Dalmuir caused delays, but the flotilla reached Bowling at the end of three exhilarating days. A strong wind was blowing, but the crowds hung around in the gathering gloom until the fish limped in and the speeches were over. It was a triumph.

Two weeks later, on 12 June 2001, Prince Charles came to the new sea lock on the River Carron and reversed the opening ceremony of 1790 by tipping a barrel of water from the Clyde into the Forth. The Forth & Clyde had been reopened, twice, and boats had passed from Grangemouth to Bowling and back again. It was a dream come true. Another dream came true on 25 August 2001 when a flotilla of boats sailed from Calders Crescent to Kingsknowe to celebrate the reopening of the Union Canal through Wester Hailes.

The Falkirk Wheel was turned for the first time on 11 December 2001, with a ceremonial opening scheduled for the end of May 2002. The canals of central Scotland had made a spectacular recovery and staked their place amongst the country's leading tourist attractions.

Children helped to open locks when the canal was operational 40 years earlier and they did it again when it reopened in May 2001—how did they remember?

Assembling the gondolas on the Falkirk Wheel, September 2001.

Bibliography

General Bibliography

Allan, J.K., *Their is a Cannal*, Falkirk Museums, 1977.

Bailey, Geoff, *Locks, Stocks and Bodies in Barrels*, Falkirk Council Library Services, 2000.

Bowman, A.I., *Swifts & Queens*, Strathkelvin District Libraries & Museums, 1984.

Bowman, A.I., *The Gipsy o' Kirky*, Strathkelvin District Libraries & Museums, 1987.

Bowman, A.I., *Kirkintilloch Shipbuilding*, Strathkelvin District Libraries & Museums, 1983.

Campbell, R.H., *Carron Company*, Oliver & Boyd, 1961.

Forrester, D.A.R., *The Great Canal that Linked Edinburgh, Glasgow and London*, Strathclyde Convergencies, 1979.

Forth & Clyde Canal Society, *The Forth & Clyde Canal Guidebook*, 3rd edition, East Dunbartonshire Libraries, 2001. (1st ed. 1985; 2nd ed. 1991)

Gladwin, D.D., *Passenger Boats on Inland Waterways*, Oakwood Press, 1979.

Gray, A., Currie, R., and Livingstone, S. *The Forth & Clyde Canal*, education pack, Strathclyde Regional Council.

Hume, John, *Industrial Archaeology of Glasgow*, Blackie, 1974.

Lindsay, Jean, *The Canals of Scotland*, David and Charles, 1968.

Martin, Don, *The Forth & Clyde Canal, a Kirkintilloch View*, Strathkelvin District Libraries & Museums, 1977.

Martin, Don, and Maclean, A.A., *Edinburgh & Glasgow Railway Guidebook*, Strathkelvin District Libraries & Museums, 1992.

Massey, Alison, *The Edinburgh and Glasgow Union Canal*, Falkirk District Council Libraries and Museums, 1983.

Pratt, E.A., *Scottish Canals and Waterways*, Selwyn and Blount, 1922.

Ransom, P.J.G., *Scotland's Inland Waterways*, NMS Publishing, 1999.

Scott, Ian, *The Life and Times of Falkirk*, John Donald, 1994.

Thomson, George, *The Monkland Canal*, Monklands Library Services Department.

Watters, Brian, *Where Iron Runs Like Water*, John Donald, 1998.

Woodside & North Kelvin Local History Project, *Scotland's Grand Canal*, 1988.

Booklets, Leaflets and Articles

Anon., *A Companion for Canal Passengers Betwixt Edinburgh and Glasgow*, reprinted by Linlithgow Union Canal Society, 1981.

British Waterways Scotland, *Union Canal*, three leaflets: *Fountainbridge to Wester Hailes, Wester Hailes to the M8, The M8 to the Avon Aqueduct*.

British Waterways with Central Regional Council and Falkirk District Council, leaflet – *The Canals of Falkirk*.

British Waterways with Strathkelvin District Council, leaflet – *The Forth & Clyde Canal in Strathkelvin District*.

Carter, Paul, *Cruising on the Gipsy Princess*, Forth & Clyde Canal Society, 1997.

Gillespie, Douglas, *Scots Magazine*, August & September 1973.

Hume, John, *The Forth & Clyde Canal*, exhibition booklet for University of Strathclyde travelling exhibition, 1979.

Linlithgow Union Canal Society, Museum Guide.

Skinner, B.C., *The Union Canal, A Report*, Linlithgow Union Canal Society, 1977.

Strathclyde Leisure and Recreation Department, *Discovering Strathclyde*, folders of leaflets; *The Forth & Clyde Canal Bishopbriggs to Wyndford* & *Bowling to Castlecary*.

Specific Bibliography and References

Chapter 1

Canal Company records held by the National Archives of Scotland, West Register House, filed under BR/FCN.

Skempton, A.W., *John Smeaton FRS*, Thomas Telford Ltd., 1981.

1   Matheson, Graham, article on Robert Mackell, *Falkirk Herald* 20/9/1952.

2   Paxton, Roland, *Luggie Aqueduct, Kirkintilloch on the Forth & Clyde Canal*, An Historical Engineering Assessment, 1992.

3   *Caledonian Mercury* 8/4/1790.

4   *Glasgow Advertiser* 26-30 July, 23-27 August 1790.

5   *Glasgow Advertiser* shipping lists, various dates, 1801.

6   *Glasgow Advertiser* 6-10 September 1790.

7   *Glasgow Courier* 20/6/1816; 2/12/1817; 28/3/1820.

8   *Glasgow Advertiser* 13-17 September 1790.

9   *Glasgow Advertiser* 18-22 February 1793; 12/12/1794.

10   *Glasgow Courier* 26/12/1816; 21/11/1818.

11   Hume, John, article Canal's Glasgow Branch, *F&C Canal News* No. 10, April 1982.

Hume, John, article Port Dundas, *Heritage* No. 39, February 1979.

12   *Glasgow Advertiser* 2/11/1798.

13   Hutton, G., Glasgow's Canal Volunteers, *Canal & Riverboat*, December 1989.

14   *Glasgow Courier* 18/10/1803; 14/1/1804.

15   *Glasgow Advertiser* 10-14 January, 8-11 July 1791.

16 *Glasgow Courier* 28/6/1814; 22/6/1815; 16/5, 20/6/1816.

17 Bowman, A.I., *Symington and the Charlotte Dundas*, Falkirk District Council Libraries and Museums, 1981.
Glasgow Courier 31/3/1803.
Glasgow Herald & Advertiser 7/1/1803.

18 *Glasgow Advertiser* 14-17 May 1790.

19 *Glasgow Advertiser* 3-7 January 1791.

20 *Glasgow Courier* 17/6/1813.

21 *Glasgow Courier* 20/5/1819.

Chapter 2

Canal Company records held by the National Archives of Scotland, West Register House filed under BR/EGU.

Handley, James E., *The Navvy in Scotland*, Cork University Press, 1970.

Skinner, Basil, Scottish Society for Industrial Archaeology newsletter, April 1970.

Worling, M.J., *Early Railways of the Lothians*, Midlothian District Libraries, 1991.

1 Rennie, John, Report concerning the different lines surveyed by John Ainslie & Robert Whitworth.
Grieve, John, & Taylor, James, Report of Canal between Edinburgh & Glasgow.
Stevenson, Robert, Report relative to a line of canal between Edinburgh & Glasgow.
Baird, Hugh, Report on the proposed Edinburgh & Glasgow Union Canal.

2 *Edinburgh Evening Courant* 5/3, 9/3/1818.

3 *Edinburgh Evening Courant* 24/1/1818.

4 Edinburgh College of Commerce, *The Union Canal and Aqueduct Bridge at Slateford*, 1970.
Glasgow Courier 27/6/1820.

5 West Lothian Library HQ, *Antiquarian Notes & Queries* vol. 3 pp 88-94.

6 *Glasgow Courier* 16/7/1818; 3/8/1820.

7 Allan, J.K., *Their is a Cannal*, Falkirk Museums, 1977.

8 *Glasgow Courier* 21/11/1818.

9 *Edinburgh Evening Courant* 12/12/1822.

10 *Edinburgh Evening Courant* 10/10/1818.
Glasgow Courier 2/9/1820.

11 *Glasgow Courier* 10/8/1820.
The Link, the Millennium Link newsletter, No. 7 Summer 1998.

12 *Glasgow Courier* 11/1, 18/8, 13/11/1821.

13 *Glasgow Courier* 3/1/1822.

14 *Edinburgh Evening Courant* 24/1/1822.

15 *Edinburgh Evening Courant* 4/3/1822.

16 *Edinburgh Evening Courant* 30/3, 8/4, 13/4/1822.

17 *Glasgow Courier* & *Edinburgh Evening Courant* 9/5/1822.

18 *Edinburgh Evening Courant* 4/5, 22/5, 13/7, 23/11/1822.

19 *Further Rules, Orders & By-Laws*, W. Lothian Library HQ.

20 *Glasgow Sentinel* 14/8/1822.

21 *Edinburgh Evening Courant* 16/11/1822.

22 *Glasgow Courier* 18/9, 12/12/1822; 7/1/1823.

Chapter 3

Canal Company records held by the National Archives of Scotland, West Register House filed under BR/FCN & BR/EGU.

Clark, Sylvia, *The Paisley Canal and its famous Iron Boats*, Old Paisley Society, 1985.

Martin, Don, *The Garnkirk & Glasgow Railway*, Strathkelvin District Council Libraries & Museums, 1981.

Martin, Don, *The Monkland & Kirkintilloch and Associated Railways*, Strathkelvin District Council Libraries & Museums, 1995.

McEwan, J.F., article Scottish Canal Railways, *Stevenson Locomotive Society Journal*, March 1972.

1 Dott, George, *Early Scottish Colliery Wagonways*, 1947.
Royal Commission on the Ancient and Historical Monuments of Scotland, *Muirkirk, Ayrshire, An Industrial Landscape*: Broadsheet No. 1.

2 Forth and Cart Canal file, Clydebank Library.
Glasgow Courier 2/8/1838; 30/5/1840.

3 Glasgow City Archives T-CN14/103/104/105.

4 *Glasgow Courier* 14/2/1837.

5 *Edinburgh Evening Courant* 26/8/1839.

6 Article published by the *St James Gazette*, reprinted in the *Kirkintilloch Herald* 23 January 1889.

Chapter 4

Bremner, David, *The Industries of Scotland*, Adam and Charles Black, 1869.

Carvel, John L., *One Hundred Years in Timber*, Brownlee and Company, 1949.

Douglas, Graham, and Oglethorpe, Miles, *Brick, Tile and Fireclay Industries in Scotland*, Royal Commission on the Ancient and Historical Monuments of Scotland, 1993.

Drummond, Peter, and Smith, James, *Coatbridge; Three Centuries of Change*, Monklands Library Services Department, 2nd, revised ed. 1984.

Kerr, David, *Shale Oil: Scotland*, author, 1988.

Oakley, C.A., ed., *Scottish Industry*, The Scottish Council (Development and Industry), 1953.

Payne, Peter L., *Growth & Contraction; Scottish Industry 1860-1990*, The Economic & Social History Society of Scotland, 1992.

Smart, Aileen, *Villages of Glasgow* vol. 1, John Donald, 1988.

Thomson, Alexander, *Random Notes etc. of Maryhill 1750–1894*, Kerr & Richardson, 1895.

1 BR/EGU/4/6/13.

2 Skillen, Brian S., *The Mines & Minerals of Bishopbriggs and District*, East Dunbartonshire Education & Leisure Services, 2000.
Skillen, Brian S., *The Mines and Minerals of Campsie*, Strathkelvin District Libraries, 1985.

3 *West Lothian Courier* 17/6/1893, 19/8/1949; *Kirkintilloch Herald* 16/1/1929.

4 *West Lothian Courier* 7/4/1950.

5 *West Lothian Courier* 23/2/1878.

6 *Glasgow Advertiser* 6-10 June 1791.
Glasgow Courier 17/1/1818.

7   Barnard, Alfred, *The Whisky Distilleries of the United Kingdom*, 1887.

    Barnard, Alfred, *Noted Breweries of Great Britain & Ireland* vol. 2, 1889.

8   Falkirk Museums, Callendar House, A053.063; A053.060/01. *Kirkintilloch Herald* 2/10/1889.

9   *Falkirk Herald* 10/11/1973.

10 King, Elspeth, *Scotland Sober & Free*, Glasgow Museums and Art Galleries, 1979

11 *Glasgow Courier* 20/5/1856.

12 *Glasgow Courier* 23/9/1809.

13 Black, William B., research paper, *The Glasgow Canal Shipbuilders*, 2000.

    Bowman, A.I., Shipyards of the Forth & Clyde Canal, *F&C Canal News* No. 8, November 1981.

    Bowman, A.I., Kelvin Dock – Birthplace of a Puffer, *F&C Canal News* No. 20, April 1984.

    Cubbage, Olive, Old Tam's Dry Dock, *F&C Canal News* No. 54, August 1991.

Chapter 5

McDonald, Dan, *The Clyde Puffer*, David & Charles, 1977.

1   *Glasgow Advertiser* 24/4/1858.

2   Black, William B., research paper, *The Glasgow Canal Shipbuilders*, 2000.

    Bowman, A.I., Shipyards of the Forth & Clyde Canal, *F&C Canal News* No. 8, November 1981.

3   Falkirk Museums, Callendar House, A 053.008.

4   *Glasgow Courier* 7/1/1792.

    Glasgow News 4/1/1875.

    Kirkintilloch Herald 6/3/1895.

5   *Glasgow Courier* 2/4/1795.

6   *Scotsman* 10/3/1827.

7   *Falkirk Herald* 14/3/1850.

    Glasgow Herald 8/9/1928.

    Kirkintilloch Herald 1/12/1897; 26/12/1900.

8   *Falkirk Herald* 24/1/1874.

    Kirkintilloch Herald 18/8/1893; 29/9/1897; 24/7, 20/11/1901; 4/5/1904; 20/3/1918; 22/9/1920.

9   *Falkirk Herald* 6/2, 27/2, 6/3, 13/31897.

    Glasgow Herald 5/2/1897.

10 *Kirkintilloch Herald* 13/3, 21/12/1895; 23/3/1898; 16/9/1903; 6/1/1904.

11 *Kirkintilloch Herald* 27/8/1898.

12 Glasgow City Archives TD 1301.

    Worsdall, Frank, *The City That Disappeared*, Richard Drew Publishing, 1981.

13 *Glasgow Herald* 26/9, 28/9, 29/9/1904.

    Kirkintilloch Herald 6/4, 4/5, 28/9, 5/10, 12/10, 19/10, 26/10, 9/11, 16/11/1904.

14 *Kirkintilloch Herald* 6/2/1907.

15 *Kirkintilloch Herald* 1/6/1892.

16 *Kirkintilloch Herald* 20/11/1895; 19/10, 27/10/1897; 11/7/1906; 19/6/1912.

Chapter 6

Bowman, A.I., Crews of the Gipsy Queen, *F&C Canal News* No. 43, May 1989.

Crerar, Catherine, A Trip Along the Canal for Only Half-a-Crown, *F&C Canal News* No. 45, November 1989.

Langmuir, Graham, Passenger Steamers of the Forth & Clyde Canal, *F&C Canal News* No. 9, February 1982.

News cuttings file, Edinburgh City Libraries.

1   *Kirkintilloch Herald* 26/4/1893.

2   *Kirkintilloch Herald* 11/6/1890; 26/6/1901.

3   *Kirkintilloch Herald* 7/8/1901.

4   *Edinburgh Evening News* 13/11/1943; 6/5/1953.

5   *Edinburgh Evening News* 30/4/1954.

6   Falkirk Museums, Callendar House, A053.060/01.

7   *Evening Despatch* 19/5/1952.

8   *Edinburgh Evening News* 17/10/1953.

9   *Kirkintilloch Herald* 10/5/1911; 26/12/1917.

10 *Kirkintilloch Herald* 16/9/1903.

11 Falkirk Museums, Callendar House, A009.003/09.

12 *Kirkintilloch Herald* 5/6/1940.

Chapter 7

News cuttings file, Edinburgh City Libraries.

Smith, W.A.C., and Anderson, Paul, *An Illustrated History of Glasgow's Railways*, Irwell Press, 1993.

Smith, W.A.C., and Anderson, Paul, *An Illustrated History of Edinburgh's Railways*, Irwell Press, 1995.

1   *Glasgow Herald* 2/8/1872.

2   *Glasgow Herald* 13/4–26/4/1882.

3   *Clydebank Press* 30/10, 27/11/1914; 12/2/1915.

    Glasgow Herald 17/2/1916.

4   *F&C Canal News* No. 55, December 1991.

    Glasgow Herald 22/1/1883.

5   *Glasgow Herald* 23/9, 5/10/1908.

6   Falkirk Museums, Callendar House, A053. 063; A053.060/01.

7   *Weekly Scotsman* 26/10/1912.

8   *Kirkintilloch Herald* 27/1/1915.

9   *Bulletin* 18/8/1916.

    Daily Record 18/8/1916.

    Evening Times 17/8/1916.

    Glasgow Herald 17/8/1916.

10 Account of Admiralty Oil Fuel Pipe Line connecting Clyde and Forth, HMSO, 1919.

11 *Kirkintilloch Herald* 8/1, 22/1/1919.

12 *Kirkintilloch Herald* 6/12/1922; 26/8/1925; 28/9, 19/10/1927; 11/1, 8/2/1928.

13 *Kirkintilloch Herald* 15/6, 22/6/1921.

14 *Kirkintilloch Herald* 10/12/1930; 2/11/1932; 7/6/1933.

15 *Edinburgh Evening News* 21/1/1933.

16 Jeffrey, Andrew, *This Time of Crisis*, Mainstream Publishing, 1993.
    Map of bomb locations, Clydebank Library.

MacPhail, I.M.M., *The Clydebank Blitz*, Clydebank Libraries and Museums Department, 1974.

17 *West Lothian Courier* 1/5/1942.

Chapter 8

Bolton, David, *Race Against Time*, Methuen, 1990.

Inland Waterways Amenity Advisory Council, Scottish Waterways; A Report to the Secretary of State for the Environment, 1974.

Lomax, E.S., article on the Union Canal, *Glasgow Herald* 21/4/1960.

News cuttings file, Edinburgh City Libraries.

Petrie, Gordon, Along Our Canal, series of articles in *Edinburgh Evening News*, 9/1976.

Rolt, L.T.C., *Narrow Boat*, Eyre Methuen, first published 1944 plus reprints.

1 *Falkirk Herald* 16/4, 23/4/1955.
   Glasgow Herald 30/12/1953; 22/3/1956.
2 *Glasgow Herald* 29/7/1958.
   IWA Bulletin No. 57, October 1958.
3 *Glasgow Herald* 22/3/1950.
4 *Glasgow Herald* 10/8, 18/8, 15/11/1950.
5 *Glasgow Herald* 19/7, 13/8, 6/9, 9/12, 10/12/1952.
6 *Glasgow Herald* 13/10/1953; 3/8/1956; 29/3/1958.
7 *Edinburgh Evening News* 7/7/1954.
   Evening Despatch 7/3/1951.
   Glasgow Herald 21/7/1953; 26/1/1955.
8 *Glasgow Herald* 3/2/1953.
9 *Edinburgh Evening News* 11/8/1959.
   Glasgow Herald 26/4/1958.
   IWA Bulletin No. 56, July 1958.

10 *Glasgow Herald* 24/2/1959.
11 *Falkirk Herald* 10/6, 25/11, 9/12/1961.
    Glasgow Herald 7/6/1961.
    IWA Bulletin No. 64, June 1961.
12 *Glasgow Herald* 9/6, 13/6, 16/6/1961; 9/4/1962.
13 *Glasgow Herald* 10/12/1962.
    IWA Bulletin No. 68, May 1963.
14 *Glasgow Herald* 12/7/1963; 5/3, 22/8/1964; 6/8/1966; 2/3/1968; 2/9/1969.
    IWA Bulletin No. 70, March 1964.
    IWA Bulletin No. 71, June 1964.
15 *Falkirk Herald* 11/4, 19/12/1964.
16 *West Lothian Courier* 26/2/1960.
17 *IWA Bulletin* No. 69, November 1963.
18 *Glasgow Herald* 12/1/1967.
19 *Glasgow Herald* 19/11/1970.
20 *Glasgow Herald* 25/4, 29/4, 11/11/1970.
    Scotsman 7/1/1972.
    West Lothian Courier 9/1/1970.
21 *Glasgow Herald* 31/10, 6/11/1969; March/May (various dates) 1973.
22 *Glasgow Herald* 14/3/1970.

Chapter 9

British Waterways Board, leaflet on The Glasgow Canal Project.

Countryside Commission for Scotland; Union Canal, Report of a Two Year Project 1979–81.

Forth & Clyde Canal Society Newsletter, *Canal News,* No. 1 June 1980 – No. 67 December 1994.

News cuttings file, Edinburgh City Libraries.

Petrie, Gordon, Along Our Canal, series of articles in *Edinburgh Evening News*, Sept. 1976.

Scottish Inland Waterways Association Newsletter (later editions Heritage) No. 1 February 1972 – No. 42 February 1980.

Strathclyde Regional Council and Falkirk District Council, Forth & Clyde Canal Local Plan, 1987 (also preceding documents).

1 *Glasgow Herald* 17/6, 26/10/1971.
2 *West Lothian Courier* 10/3/1972.
3 *West Lothian Courier* 6/10/1972.
4 *Edinburgh Evening News* 28/6/1974.
5 Chadwick, Tom, *Scots Magazine*, May 1981.
6 *Glasgow Herald* 19/8/1972.

Chapter 10

Forth & Clyde Canal Society Newsletter, *Canal News*, No. 67 December 1994 – No. 102 December 2001.

The Link, newsletters for the Millennium Link 1994–2002.

Bridge Blethers

1 Ellis, Peter Beresford, and Mac a' Ghobhainn, Seamas, *The Scottish Insurrection of 1820*, Pluto Press, 1989.
2 *Glasgow Courier* 11/11/1819.
3 *Glasgow Weekly Mail* 15/1/1910.

4 *Daily Record* 20/7/1955.
5 *Kirkintilloch Herald* 25/3/1942.
6 *Glasgow Herald* 31/7/1947.

Index

Nº 2. VIEW IN CALLENDAR PARK, SITUATE IN THE C

Taken from the same point as Nº 1. shewn

Parliamentary Line of the Edinburgh and